SCHOCKEN LIBRARY / 12

FERDINAND GREGOROVIUS

The Ghetto and the Jews of Rome

SCHOCKEN BOOKS / NEW YORK

"TEMPLE ISRAEL"

COPYRIGHT 1948 BY SCHOCKEN BOOKS INC.
342 MADISON AVENUE, NEW YORK 17, N. Y.

Translated by Moses Hadas

"Lament of the Children of Israel in Rome"
translated by Randall Jarrell

Manufactured in the U.S.A. by H. Wolff, New York

"THIS tiny Jewish colony has seen the Roman Republic and the Empire fall; it has wept at Caesar's death; it has seen the Barbarians come; it has seen everything change and the Church build herself. And at the beginning of the century it is still there, having merely, in the course of two thousand years, crossed the Tiber."

The wonder and perplexity expressed by Bernard Lazare at the turn of the nineteenth century had, fifty years before, in 1853, prompted the German historian Ferdinand Gregorovius to write the essay and poem that follow. He was profoundly moved by the identity of spirit and uninterrupted life of an ancient people, by an isolation which had been a self-assumed goal as well as a physical imposition from without; and yet, though moved, he observed this phenomenon and traced its outlines with the detached curiosity of the outsider.

It is likely that the history of no other Jewish locality in Europe would have struck the non-Jewish historian with such an impression of timelessness, since none was so strangely bare of great spiritual events and significant activity as that of the ghetto in Rome, with its unique life in the shadow of the Eternal City under the heavy impact of the center of Catholic Christianity.

Contents

LAMENT OF THE CHILDREN OF ISRAEL IN ROME   11

THE GHETTO AND THE JEWS OF ROME   19

TRANSLATOR'S POSTSCRIPT   109

CHRONOLOGICAL TABLE   115

Lament of the Children of Israel in Rome

VERY bitter were the sorrows
Of our fathers, who in exile
Hung their harps upon the weeping
Willows of the flat Euphrates:
But beside the Tiber's flood,
Pressed behind these stifling gratings,
We hang up our wailing's zither;
Judah's children, we—in Rome.

We last children of those slaves
The Romans led here, once, from Canaan,
In their triumph over Zion—
Those who sank waist-deep in shame;
We orphans of the Holy City
Build forever, stone on stone,
Our own pyramid of sorrow
Here above the Roman rubble.

For two thousand years we mourned
Beside this stream, whose yellow waves
Rush savagely, in wild confusion,
Past the ghetto's dreary walls;
With our fathers' wailing courage,
One in grief, we have endured:
We weep, as they have wept,
Eternally, to this same stream.

Nation after nation fell;
But we cling, like the undying
Green ivy to these ruins—cling
To Octavia's shattered halls,
The witnesses of our dishonor
When our motherland's despoiler,
When Jerusalem's destroyer
Stood to judge the seed of Judah.

Alas! for us, in narrow alleys,
In rooms the sunlight could not reach—
Not even fit to hold our anguish—
Pharaoh piled another Goshen;
And there came to gape upon us,
To mock our bitter agony
Sneering Brothers, haughty Fathers,
In their glances hate and death.

So we sigh, and sew the tatters
In this rubbish of the Romans,
And we think: As this has shattered,
So Rome must also—and must perish.
But we still, in mockery,
Cling fast, like the undying
Green ivy to the ruins—
For, alas, it is a ruin!

No more, from the Arch of Titus,
Can the marble pictures grieve us:
Candlesticks, the Temple's tablets,
And the Jordan's holy waters;
Long ago, in filth and dust,
Thy gods, O Rome, have perished—
But Jehovah's holy emblems
Shine forth after a thousand years.

The grass springs above the rubble
Of the temple of the Father, Jove;
And down into the dust have fallen
The palaces of every Caesar:
But here, in spite of Time and Death,
To Thine everlasting glory
Thine old altars rise unbroken—
Lord of Times, of Life, Jehovah!

By the waters of the Tiber
We set up, with silent weeping,
Poorly, and with unhewn stones,
The sanctuary of Thy temple;
And we traced upon the walls
Thine emblems, Lord, that we might still
Remember, when they met our gaze,
Thy house's old magnificence.

And we sons of Abraham,
The faithful brotherhood, have met
Once more, before the Holy Ark,
In the Sabbath's quiet hour;
And we bear before the face
Of Elohim, the seven fold
Light of the seven fold lamp—
The unchanged, undying light.

Then we chorus, with the tongues
Of our fathers, to the harps,
In harmonies our sorrow sharpens,
David's Psalms, still unforgotten:
Till the tears begin to flow—
And once more, from our hearts,
The pain of a thousand years
Melts into hope for the Messiah.

Like the Messenger who passes
Through the streets, to chalk the marks
Of death upon the houses: Here
And here they die; so fever wanders—
Plague on plague, in their full power,
Dread and toil at every hour,
And our shame—all bound together
With the gnawing ache of hunger.

In the street outside, the laughing
Crowds surge, packed from wall to wall,
And the gay floats roll among
The masked and glittering throngs;
In its gold-embroidered silk
Each house is dressed for holiday—
From balcony and window, Joy
Strews, as spring strews, flowers, flowers.

Then the roses—ah! of Sharon
We remember: how they withered,
How the blossoms fell in clusters
From the almond-wand of Aaron.
Zion's daughter, stripped of jewels,
Maid of Rome: into the ashes
You must bow your head, in silence—
In a silence full of tears.

We think of our abandoned daughters.
We remember how the lashes
Scourged our fathers to their judgment
Through the people's mocking laughter.
We think how the blood of Judah
Stained the threshold of St. Peter's.
We see, still, the livid frightful
Glare of the flames about the stake.

Now, in the sweat of our faces,
Day after day, we sit before
Our doorsteps; and all our toil
Lengthens with our bitter zeal—
And from every hole and corner
We hunt out our rags and patches,
For with loathing hands, the world
Throws us its refuse, only.

Alas, the rags make us remember
Solomon: all earthly glory
Breaks to pieces—and at last,
Like these rags here, falls to nothing.
Oh, the bracelets that adorned you,
Zion's daughters! All are gone,
All your glittering dress is tarnished,
All that was is rags and tatters.

The Ghetto and the Jews of Rome

SQUEEZED into a dismal and depressing corner of the city of Rome, across the Tiber from Trastevere, Rome's Jewry lives as it has from antiquity, virtually shut off from humanity. This Jewry is the subject matter of these pages, which the author has put together from writings ancient and modern and from oral communications of the Hebrews themselves. He has frequently wandered through Rome's ghetto, and its people have seemed to him notable among the city's antiquities, for they are Rome's only living ruins and as such merit our careful consideration.

Perhaps the majority of foreigners who make the pilgrimage to Rome's monuments are most deeply stirred by the triumphal Arch of Titus in the Forum. Its significance is easiest for them to grasp because the history of the Jews and of Jerusalem their city is part of the Christian's native heritage and engages his sympathy. The frieze of the Arch still shows the triumphal procession, the sacred river Jordan figured as a venerable man being borne upon a barrow. In the passageway of the Arch, through which no Jew will pass, the holy vessels of the Temple at Jerusalem which were carried in Titus' triumphal procession are to be distinguished: the seven-branched candelabrum, the golden table of the shewbread, the Ark in which the Law was kept, and the silver trumpets of the jubilee. Almost eighteen hundred years have elapsed since the Arch was erected, and nothing is left of that Rome which ruled the world but ruins and dust and the symbols of a remote cult, having no connection with living things. If we descend from the Arch of Titus toward the Tiber and wander through the ghetto, we notice the seven-branched candelabrum engraved here and there on the walls of the inhabited houses. It is the same design which we just now saw on the Arch, but here it is alive as a functioning symbol of the Jewish religion and to this day there dwell in these houses descendants of the Jews whom Titus once led in triumph. If we visit the synagogue of the Hebrews we see the same sculptures of the Ark of the Covenant, the golden table, the jubilee trumpet, decorating its walls. Beneath the figures of the Temple vessels which Titus once brought to Rome, the Jewish people, still persisting, still undestroyed, offers up its prayers to the ancient Jehovah of Jerusalem. Jehovah has proved more powerful than the Capitoline Jupiter.

Here is the Porticus of Octavia. Its great arches and pillars, now dilapidated and obstructed by buildings, tower high hard by the ghetto. It was here that Vespasian and Titus once with festive pomp inaugurated the march of triumph over Israel. A Jew stood by that day to observe the festivities, Flavius Josephus, the well-known historian, companion and flatterer of Titus. He was not ashamed to participate in the triumph over his own people, to revel in the splendor of the display, and to describe it with fulsome flattery. It is to this contemptible court Jew that we owe the description of the triumph.

"The military, while night still reigned, had all marched out in companies and divisions, under their commanders, and been drawn up, not round the doors of the upper palace, but near the temple of Isis; for there the emperors reposed that night. At the break of dawn, Vespasian and Titus issued forth, crowned with laurel and clad in the traditional purple robes, and proceeded to the Octavian walks; for here the senate and the chief magistrates and those of equestrian rank were awaiting their coming. A tribunal had been erected in front of the porticoes, with chairs of ivory placed for them upon it; to these they mounted and took their seats. Instantly acclamations rose from the troops, all bearing ample testimony to their valour: the princes were unarmed, in silk robes and crowned with bays. Vespasian, having acknowledged their acclamations, which they wished to prolong, made the signal for silence; then amidst profound and universal stillness he rose and, covering most of his head with his mantle, recited the customary prayers, Titus also praying in like manner. After the prayers, Vespasian, having briefly addressed the assembled company, dismissed the soldiers to the customary breakfast provided for them by the emperors, and himself withdrew to the gate which, in consequence of the triumphal processions always passing through it, has thence derived its name. Here the princes first partook of refreshment, and then, having donned their triumphal robes and sacrificed to the gods whose statues stood beside the gate, they sent the pageant on its way, driving off through the theatres, in order to give the crowds an easier view." *

Augustus had built the magnificent Porticus with its double colonnade to honor his sister Octavia. A part of the propylaea is still preserved. It is hard by the fish market which borders the ghetto. Built into its ruins is the church of Sant' Angelo in Pescaria, a church which likewise is

* Josephus *Jewish War* (translation of H. St. J. Thackeray) vii. 123-31.

related to the Jews because in it they were compelled to listen to weekly conversionist sermons. And so the ghetto is situated next to that Porticus of Octavia where Vespasian and Titus dedicated their triumph over the Jews, and around the same Porticus, now a mass of filth, live today the descendants of those Hebrews who were once Titus' captives and slaves.

Because of the historical relation of the people of Israel to the Romans, who destroyed Jerusalem and dispersed the Jews over the world, the ghetto of Rome is the most remarkable of all the Jewish communities of Europe. Other Jewries, especially those of Spain and Portugal in the Middle Ages and of the synagogue of Amsterdam which derives from them, are more notable for their scholarly and theological attainments but none is of such antiquity and of such altogether historical immediacy as the Jewry of Rome. Neither Talmud nor Jewish philosophy nor Kabbalah could flourish in this locality, for the ghetto of Rome is virtually another Goshen of Pharaonic slavery; its history is that of the almost incredible obstinacy of a small slave community enduring an oppression which persisted from generation to generation.

When we reflect that it is in Rome that this

Jewry has maintained itself for eighteen centuries, its resistance excites astonishment. It might almost seem an enigma that this abused group, for the greater part descended from the same exhausted strain —though renewed and strengthened by fresh increments—was able to persist from generation to generation through the centuries in the very same narrow alleyways, in the very same pestilential air, and maintain itself as an individual and living organism. For Jews have lived in Rome since the time of Pompey the Great. Upon several occasions expelled from the city by the early emperors, they always returned, and from the time of Titus to this day they have retained their residence in the city, making their home in what for them was the most dangerous spot in the world because it was in sight first of their enemies, the Romans who had destroyed Jerusalem, and afterward of the popes, the vicars of Christ whom the Jews had crucified. From Pompey's time onward they were abused and despised, and finally like unclean pariahs organized into a ghetto; they clung together in a cramped corner, now no longer exposed to the wild beasts as in Claudius' day, but to the injurious prejudices of the Christians. They survived all the vicissitudes of the centuries and the fearful monotony of their own condition—a grim spectacle and a dark page in the annals of Christian humanity. They lived hopeless and yet not without hope, as is appropriate for Israel, to whom the prophets promised a Messiah. Incapable of confronting their enemies by bold offense, they fortified themselves behind the strongest and saddest weapon of misery—habit and the tenacity of Jewish family life. Their power to endure—albeit through slavery the Jews have grown more servile than all other slaves—is so remarkable that I confess I cannot explain it. A man of character is sustained in misery by his moral dignity, a philosopher by his philosophy, a Christian by his Christianity which has peopled heaven with martyrs and has planted the cross in the paradise of the blessed. But Jehovah gives the Jews nothing beyond the grave, and they have no saints.

Whatever be the source of this power to endure, the power is a fact, and it appears that nature itself has provided the most wretched of all human groups with the most vigorous impulse to survive. Under similar conditions in Rome, perhaps any other people would have perished, incapable of enduring the world's boundless contempt. But the Jews could endure it, and through all the centuries they maintained themselves at the very center of Catholic Christianity and under the very feet of the popes. Excluded from all civic intercourse with their fellow men, they never intermarried with the Romans; their latest descendants are as alien to the city's Christians as were their earliest ancestors, and they are no nearer to the Romans than they were in the time of Pompey. Then, and later under the emperors, though despised, they were regarded as one among the Oriental sects from Syria, Egypt, and Persia, and consequently they were not so isolated as today; for they alone out of the confusion of the countless religious sects of ancient Rome have remained alive and unchanged.

To construct a history of the Jews of Rome such as will here be briefly attempted is difficult, at least for the early period, for the reports of the Roman writers are rather scanty.

With Pompey's entry into Jerusalem, where out of curiosity and despite the petitions of the horrified Jews he even entered the Holy of Holies, there begins an enduring connection between Jerusalem and Rome. Pompey appears to have brought the first Jewish slaves to Rome; it is certain at least that after his time Jewish freedmen and other Hebrews, apparently attracted by trade, resided in the city. Here they were free to live according to the religious usages of their Law, while the princes and princesses of their country, esteemed equally with other petty kings and princes, appeared on occasion before the senate and the court at Rome to represent their interests. For in those days there still were Jewish princes. The fortunate Herod, wearing all the insignia of royal dignity, might often be seen at Rome associating as a prince with the Caesars, dining at their table, and occupying the princes' loge in the theater. Archelaus and the Jewish princess Salome, Antipas and Antipater might be seen in the city; and not a few Jewish princes were educated at the court in Rome. Agrippa, Herod's grandson, an adventurous fortune hunter, was educated with Drusus, son of Tiberius, and was the bosom friend of Caligula, whose vices he shared. The youthful Jewish wastrel had scarcely emerged from a debtors' jail when Tiberius threw him into a dungeon where he languished for six months until the death of the Emperor liberated him and Caligula made him King of the Jews. The beautiful princess Veronica or Berenice, daughter of Agrippa, played a particularly glamorous role in Rome. She was sister and paramour of her brother the younger Agrippa, last King of the Jews. After the destruction of Jerusalem she lived in Titus' quarters as his lover, but despite all manner of intrigue she never succeeded in making herself empress of Rome. Herod Agrippa, incidentally, was the last Jew to receive marks of distinction in Rome. Since that time the Jewish community has seen none of their coreligionists honored with the exception of Baron Rothschild, who was shown high favor in the time of Gregory XVI—for reasons easy to surmise.

While adventurous Jewish princes were now and again to be seen in Rome in that period, other Jews had already settled in the city. Julius Caesar was favorable to them; this is proven by the fact that after his assassination they wept for him and chanted dirges. Augustus too gave them full liberty to move about in Rome and drive their trade; hence out of gratitude they lamented his death and bewailed him, as we are told, for a whole week. They were not at that time confined to a particular section of the city, though Philo tells us that Augustus gave the Jews of Rome the Transtiber quarter, which he says was a desirable location. They lived in other sections also, but were most numerous in modern Trastevere, that is to say not far from the present ghetto and across the river. According to Roman tradition, St. Peter sojourned in Trastevere in 45 A.D., in the vicinity of the modern Church of Santa Cecilia because Jews were living there. But he is also said to have lived on the Aventine, in the house of SS. Aquila and Prisca, a Jewish couple who had accepted Christianity.

Augustus' mild treatment of the Jews is to be deduced from a passage in Philo's very remarkable tract on the *Legatio ad Caium*. The learned Alexandrian tells us that the Emperor was always well disposed to the Jews. He knew that they inhabited the large quarter across the Tiber and that they were mostly freedmen who had been brought to Italy as captives and liberated by their masters. They were not constrained to alter their ancestral usages. A remarkable tombstone of the Via Appia which bears the names of two Jews, Zabda and Akiba, reminds us even today of such Jewish freedmen. It was known to Augustus, Philo continues, that the Jews possessed synagogues where they assembled each week to receive instruction in the doctrines of their ancestral wisdom. He even permitted them to send money for first fruits to Jerusalem, so that sacrifices might be offered there on their behalf. He neither expelled them from Rome nor deprived them of their rights as Roman citizens, for he was of a friendly mind to the Jewish people. He caused no changes to be made in their synagogues nor in their assemblies. He himself, Philo relates, enriched the Temple at Jerusalem with costly gifts and provided for sacrifices to be offered there. He regarded the Sabbath so highly that he ordered that the Jews' portion in the distribution of grain be given them not on that day but on the day following, since on that sacred day the Jews might neither receive nor give money or gifts.

We know that in 40 B.C. Philo was sent by the Jews of Alexandria to head a delegation to the Emperor Gaius (Caligula) for the purpose of making representations concerning the cruel abuses which the Alexandrians were inflicting upon the Jews, who were numerous in that emporium of world trade. He tells how Caligula received the Jewish delegation at his country house, how he scurried like a madman from one chamber to another, now giving orders for some new construction and now ordering old pictures to be set up, while the Jews followed him from chamber to chamber amidst the continuous laughter of all those present. The Emperor himself mocked them and asked why they ate no pork. "The noise of those who hooted at us," says Philo, "and of those who mocked us with their resounding laughter was as great as though we were standing in some theater." Thus even in that remote day we have the same scenes as were to be seen in Rome during the Middle Ages and in modern times, when the Jews stood in rows at Monte Giordano or at the Arch of Titus to welcome the newly chosen pope, and to be mocked all the while by the whistles of the street lads and the echoing laughter of the throngs.

Caligula had special grounds for his bitterness against the Jews. He had conceived the idea of having a colossal statue of himself in the character of a god set up in the Holy of Holies of the Temple at Jerusalem, for he had learned that the Jewish people alone among the nations of the earth had refused to grant him divine honors. He issued orders to Petronius, the governor of Phoenicia, to have the statue set up. Thereupon, as Josephus and Philo relate, all Judea, men, women, children, and the aged, betook themselves to Phoenicia. They covered the country like a cloud, and so loud was their lament that even when it ceased its echoes reverberated through the air. They threw themselves upon their knees before Petronius and adjured him to slay them all, weaponless as they were: they would never suffer the sanctuary of God to be desecrated. The scene represents one of the most magnificent tragedies a people has ever experienced, and the moral resistance they offered to Caligula is one of the most admirable episodes in the history of the Jewish people, shedding more glory upon them than the greatest achievements of David and Solomon. Petronius was deeply moved, and admonished Caligula in a letter; and now that King Agrippa who had been the friend of the Emperor's youth came to Rome to enter a petition on behalf of his people. Philo tells us that Agrippa's shock over Caligula's intentions to desecrate the Temple was so great that he was carried out in a faint and he fell into a grave illness. Finally Philo represents him as writing a masterly letter in consequence of which this ruler, to whom all the world had dedicated temples, altars, and statues, desisted from his passion to set a statue of himself up in the sanctuary at Jerusalem. His early death protected the Jews of Rome from his vengeance. But Philo, unfortunately, tells us nothing of the condition of the contemporary Jewish community across the Tiber. It appears that they formed a synagogue there, which was called the synagogue of the libertines, or freedmen.

From the time the Christian mysteries had made their way into Rome, Jews and Christians were regarded as a common sect, and the fact that the Christians were for the most part of Jewish origin favored the confusion. Hence they shared persecutions equally. In 51, Claudius expelled all of them from the city; Tiberius, upon the advice of Sejanus, had already banished them to Sardinia in order to put a stop to their disgraceful usury. This shows that even then they had turned to moneylending as their calling. But after each expulsion they returned and succeeded in maintaining themselves. Their numbers grew so that under the early emperors they were estimated at 8,000, or more than twice the number of Jews in Rome today. With the fall of Judea and the destruction of Jerusalem by Titus, crowds of Jewish captives of war were haled to Rome as slaves. Some were executed, but the greater part remained in Rome. I consider it worth-while to continue the account of the triumph, so that the reader who is unfamiliar with Flavius Josephus may have a picture of that remarkable pageant:

"It is impossible adequately to describe the multitude of those spectacles and their magnificence under every conceivable aspect, whether in works of art or diversity of riches or natural rarities; for almost all the objects which men who have ever been blessed by fortune have acquired one by one—the wonderful and precious productions of various nations—by their collective exhibition on that day displayed the majesty of the Roman empire. Silver and gold and ivory in masses, wrought into all manner of forms, might be seen, not as if carried in procession, but flowing, so to speak, like a river; here were tapestries borne along, some of the rarest purple, others embroidered by Babylonian art with perfect portraiture; transparent gems, some set in golden crowns, some in other fashions, swept by in such profusion as to correct our erroneous supposition that any of them was rare. Then, too, there were carried images of their gods, of marvellous size and no mean craftsmanship, and of these not one but was of some rich material. Beasts of many species were led along all caparisoned with appropriate trappings. The numerous attendants conducting each group of animals were decked in garments of true purple dye, interwoven with gold; while those selected to take part in the pageant itself had about them choice ornaments of amazing richness. Moreover, even among the mob of captives, none was to be seen unadorned, the variety and beauty of their dresses concealing from view any unsightliness arising from bodily disfigurement.

"But nothing in the procession excited so much

astonishment as the structure of the moving stages; indeed, their massiveness afforded ground for alarm and misgiving as to their stability, many of them being three or four stories high, while the magnificence of the fabric was a source at once of delight and amazement. For many were enveloped in tapestries interwoven with gold, and all had a framework of gold and wrought ivory. The war was shown by numerous representations, in separate sections, affording a very vivid picture of its episodes. Here was to be seen a prosperous country devastated, there whole battalions of the enemy slaughtered; here a party in flight, there others led into captivity; walls of surpassing compass demolished by engines, strong fortresses overpowered, cities with well-manned defences completely mastered and an army pouring within the ramparts, an area all deluged with blood, the hands of those incapable of resistance raised in supplication, temples set on fire, houses pulled down over their owners' heads, and, after general desolation and woe, rivers flowing, not over a cultivated land, nor supplying drink to man and beast, but across a country still on every side in flames. For to such sufferings were the Jews destined when they plunged into the war; and the art and magnificent workmanship of these structures now portrayed the incidents to those who had not witnessed them, as though they were happening before their eyes. On each of the stages was stationed the general of one of the captured cities in the attitude in which he was taken. A number of ships also followed.

"The spoils in general were borne in promiscuous heaps; but conspicuous above all stood out those captured in the Temple at Jerusalem. These consisted of a golden table, many talents in weight, and a lampstand, likewise made of gold, but constructed on a different pattern from those which we use in ordinary life. Affixed to a pedestal was a central shaft, from which there extended slender branches, arranged trident-fashion, a wrought lamp being attached to the extremity of each branch; of these there were seven, indicating the honor paid to that number among the Jews. After these, and last of all the spoils, was carried a copy of the Jewish Law. Then followed a large party carrying images of victory, all made of ivory and gold. Behind them drove Vespasian, followed by Titus; while Domitian rode beside them, in magnificent apparel and mounted on a steed that was itself a sight.

"The triumphal procession ended at the temple of Jupiter Capitolinus, on reaching which they halted; for it was a time-honored custom to wait there until the execution of the enemy's general was announced. This was Simon, son of Gioras, who had just figured in the pageant among the prisoners, and then, with a halter thrown over him and scourged meanwhile by his conductors, had been haled to the spot abutting on the Forum, where the Roman law requires that malefactors condemned to death should be executed. After the announcement that Simon was no more and the shouts of universal applause which greeted it, the princes began the sacrifices, which having been duly offered with the customary prayers, they withdrew to the palace. Some they entertained at a feast at their own table: for all the rest provision had already been made for banquets in their several homes. For the city of Rome kept festival that day for her victory in the campaign against her enemies, for the termination of her civil dissensions, and for her dawning hopes of felicity." *

Vespasian then erected a magnificent temple to Peace. This temple he endowed with the vessels of the Temple at Jerusalem, but the Ark of the Covenant and its purple hangings he deposited in the palace of the Caesars.† The triumphal arch on whose inner panels the holy vessels and the hostile

* Josephus *op. cit.* vii. 132-157.
† [The Ark of the Covenant disappeared at the destruction of the First Temple; what Vespasian deposited in the Flavian palace on the Palatine was a Scroll of the Law.—*Tr.*]

procession were depicted with such consummate art was completed only after the death of Titus. In the Middle Ages it was called because of its decoration the Arch of the Seven Lamps, or as the author of *Mirabilia Romae* puts it, *Arcus septem lucernarum Titi et Vespasiani ubi est candelabrum Moysi cum arca*. Its ancient Roman character was altered in the Middle Ages, for the powerful Frangipani, who controlled the Forum and the Colosseum, transformed it into a fortress and built upon it a tower called Turris Cartularia. It was only under Pius VII, in 1822, that the Arch was restored to the aspect it now has, one of the most noteworthy antiquities of the city and at the same time its most modern restoration.

After his triumph Titus scorned to assume the customary honorific cognomen, which would be *Judaicus*—an indication of his contempt for the Jews. But like Vespasian, he tolerated the Hebrews in Rome, who naturally increased considerably by accessions of slaves and freedmen. Vespasian granted them the free practice of their religion, but the poll tax of a half shekel which they had previously paid to the Temple treasury they were now required to pay to the Capitoline Jupiter. Even today (1853) the Jews pay their tribute to the Camera Capitolina, on the same hill. Under Domitian, as Suetonius reports, this *Fiscus Ju-*

daicus was exacted with great severity. At the time the Jews resided mostly in Trastevere, but that cruel emperor banished them from the limits of the city. Singularly enough, he assigned them the valley of Egeria, for which they were required to pay a rental. So Juvenal tells us in his third Satire:

Where Numa modell'd once the Roman state,
In mighty Councils with his Nymphs retir'd:
Tho' now the sacred Shades and Founts are hir'd
By banish'd Jews, who their whole Wealth can lay
In a small Basket, on a Wisp of Hay.
Yet such our Av'rice is, that ev'ry Tree
Pays for his Head; not sleep it self is free:
Nor Place, nor Persons, now are Sacred held,
From their own Grove the Muses are expell'd.
Into this lonely Vale our Steps we bend,
I and my sullen discontented Friend:
The Marble Caves, and Aquaeducts we view;
But how adult'rate now, and different from the true!
How much more Beauteous had the Fountain been,
Embellish'd with her first created Green,
Where Crystal Streams thro' living Turf had run,
Contented with an Urn of Native Stone.*

As he passed through the Porta Capena to the valley of Egeria, Juvenal must have seen the Jews, looking rather beggarly, it would seem, and going back and forth with trusses of hay and

* Juvenal (translation of John Dryden) iii. 12-20.

baskets, gypsy-like earning their living. The trusses served them for bedding and in the baskets they carried their poor wares and their provisions. From Roman accounts we may infer that the Jews of the time were quite similar to those of today in their character and trade. The contempt of the Romans for these unfortunate people was great, and it was considered disgraceful to have appeared in a Jewish house of prayer, whereas participation in the cult of Isis, Mithra, or Priapus was not considered shameful. Remarkably enough, Jewish worship which was always free of idols and of reverence for images and animals was treated with scorn and contempt by the Romans.

In his fourteenth Satire, Juvenal complains of the superstition which impelled Romans to accept Judaism:

The Jews, like their bigotted Sires before,
By gazing on the Clouds, their God adore:
So superstitious, that they'll sooner Dine
Upon the flesh of Men than that of Swine.
Our Roman Customs they contemn and jeer,
But learn and keep their Country-Rites with Fear.
That Worship only they in Rev'rence have,
Which in Dark Volumes their Great Moses gave.*

* *Ibid.* xiv. 96-102.

Like the gypsies among us, the Jews of that time occupied themselves with fortunetelling, with secret arts of love, and with mysterious remedies. This too Juvenal tells us, in his sixth Satire:

A Gypsie Jewess whispers in your Ear,
And begs an Alms: An High-Priest's Daughter she,
Vers'd in their Talmud and Divinity,
And prophesies beneath a shady Tree.
Her Goods a Basket, and old Hay her Bed,
She strouls, and Telling Fortunes gains her Bread:
Farthings, and some small Monies are her Fees;
Yet she Interprets all your Dreams for these.*

In these verses the satirist sketches so precise a picture of his Jewish subject that we may veritably see a gypsy jade before our very eyes. And just as in Domitian's day Jewish females silently crept out of the valley of Egeria by night in order to slip into the house of some pleasure-loving Roman lady, so the practice continued down to recent times in Rome. For many Jewish females from the ghetto crept about the town as fortunetellers, interpreting dreams for elegant ladies, selling love potions, and offering aphrodisiacs. Pius V's bull of 1569, which begins *Hebraeorum gens sola quondam a Domino electa*, has specific reference

* *Ibid.* vi. 542-547.

to this practice. This remarkable decree, by which Jews were banished from all the cities of the Church State except Rome and Ancona, is an important historical document. Though the interval of time is very great, I shall cite certain passages out of this bull for the sake of comparison with the lines in Juvenal:

"After this people lost its priesthood, after the authority of the law was taken from it, it was dispersed from its own seat which God in His mercy and lovingkindness had prepared for this people from its beginning as a land flowing with milk and honey. For many centuries now it has wandered over the face of the earth, hated and covered with all manner of scorn and contumely. It has engaged in infamous and shameful arts, in order to quiet its hunger, not otherwise than the most depraved slave society."

The document proceeds to enumerate these arts:

"To say nothing of the manifold sorts of usury by which the Jews consume the possessions of needy Christians, we believe it is quite patent that they are fences for robbers and thieves and are their accomplices, that they conceal all manner of stolen and snatched goods, not profane alone but even such as belong to divine service, either to conceal it for a time, or to transport it to another locality, or even to venture to transform its appearance so that it might no longer be recognized. Many also under the appearance of the requirements of legitimate business steal into the houses of respectable women where they incite many to abysmal lewdness. Most corrupting of all, they seduce many imprudent and weak women with satanic jugglery, with fortunetelling, wizardry, magic arts, and witchcraft; and they make these women believe that the future can be foretold, stolen articles, treasures, and hidden things be located, and withal that many things can be revealed concerning which it is not granted to any mortal to be capable of divining."

Thus the bull of Pius V. I have no doubt that even today Jewish women practice such magic arts and concoct love potions secretly in their houses.

I venture to suggest that the nature of the Hebrews themselves was responsible for the contempt, equally great at all times, with which the Jews were regarded. To the Romans their traits which bordered on caricature must have seemed ridiculous. For they are peculiar, and I may remark, with no desire to irritate either the many excellent and worthy people among the Jews nor yet the nation in general, that the European frequently finds something of caricature in the typically Jewish character, which excites ridicule just as that buffoon dance of King David before the Ark of the Covenant was most ridiculous and filled even Michal with scorn. Moreover, there was the pride of being the chosen people of God, a great and admirable destiny indeed, which is fully justified by the history of the Jewish people and their survival, unique among the peoples of the world. Finally, there was their contempt for all other faiths and their avoidance of contact with all other people. So this people began to suffer the curse of its national pride and the penalty of its castelike seclusion, until in the end it was contemptuously confined by the Christians in the menagerie of the ghetto.

The condition of the Jews in Rome under the later emperors is little known. One report tells us that Alexander Severus granted them permission to remain in Trastevere, which must have been inhabited by Jews to the end of the Middle Ages. Hadrian had destroyed Jerusalem again, this time completely, and countless Jews were sold in the markets of Syria at the price of horses. Without doubt the Jewry of Rome was considerably increased at this period.

When Christianity became the official religion of the Roman state, the position of the Jews in relation to the rulers and magistrates of Rome was sharply changed for the worse; for to the ancient Roman contempt there was now added the new hatred for the enemies of Christ. Constantine had already issued a decree forbidding Hebrews to keep Christian servants, which shows that the separation of the Jews from the Christian community had acquired a religious aspect. The Theodosian code promulgated even stricter proscriptions against their mingling with Christians. It forbade the Jews in all the provinces to celebrate a certain festival at which they were accustomed to give sly expression to their hatred for the crucified Savior. This was the festival which commemorated the fall of their enemy Haman; they represented Haman as crucified and on that day burned him in effigy amidst shouts and revelry as if he were the Christ.

As long as the senate as a merely official civic body governed the city after the fall of Rome's dominion, the lot of the Hebrews was somewhat better. But under the rule of the popes they were delivered over to a fanaticism which gradually mounted to barbarism ordained by law. Still, in the first centuries of the Middle Ages hatred of the Jews was not yet so great that the Hebrews could be regarded and treated as the offscourings of humanity. There was many a pope who gave them humane protection. Even in the time of Alexander III (1159-1185) there were free and respected Jews living in Rome, including some wealthy physicians of great repute. Benjamin of Tudela relates that there were about two hundred Jews in Rome at the time, respected and owing no man tribute, and that there were servants of the pope among them. "One may find there," he says, "very wise men, of whom the first is Rabbi Daniel. Rabbi Yehiel is minister to the Pope, a handsome lad, clever and sage, who has free access to the court of Alexander."

Even more remarkable, the Antipope Anacletus II (died 1138), by birth Pier Leone, was the grandson of a baptized Jew. For long centuries his family played a brilliant role in Rome as one of the most highly regarded patrician houses. Richly endowed with talents, as it is today, by nature and by the opposition which sharpens the intellect, bold and aggressive despite all submissiveness, this people was able to worm its way even into the inner sanctum of the papacy. While Jewish females were telling fortunes in the houses of the nobility and in the dark of night brewing love potions for smitten gentlewomen, Jews freely went to and from the needy and debt-ridden popes and became their brokers and bankers and finally their physicians. All the Jewish physicians of the popes can be found listed by name in Mandosio's work, *Degli Archiatri Pontifici*, which was brought to completion by Marini (Rome, 1784). The first in the series is Joshua Halorki, physician to the Antipope Benedict XIII (1394), who seems to have been especially friendly to the Jews. Later Halorki was baptized and called himself Hieronimus de Sancta Fede. Under this name he wrote a book against the Jews, *Hieronimi de Sancta Fede ex Judaeo Christiani contra Judaeorum perfidiam et Talmud tractatus, sive libri duo ad mandatum D. PP. Benedicti XIII*. His name was execrated by the synagogue, like that of Uriel Acosta. Innocent VII, whose Antipope Benedict was, gave some Jews of Trastevere the rights of Roman citizenship in 1406; included were Master Elijah di Sabbato, Master Moses di Bisbona, and Master Moses di Tivoli, all physicians. As such they enjoyed great privileges, and were excused from wearing the insulting Jews' badge. The personal physician of Martin V Colonna (1417-1431) was Elijah, of the ghetto of Rome. Till well into the sixteenth century Jewish personal physicians are met with in the Vatican, despite all bulls of expulsion issued by one or another hostile pope. As Orientals and as kin of the Arabs the Jews were esteemed for medical science the world over, even among princes and emperors. Samuel Sarfadi (Zarfati), a Spanish rabbi, was Leo X's physician and a thoroughly scholarly and eloquent man. Naturally, a reflection of papal favor when the Jewish physician enjoyed it, reverted to the Jews in Trastevere. But the character of Church government was personal and so the lot of Roman Jewry depended entirely upon the attitude of the pope in office. Varying treatment kept them constantly on the alert, fed their hopes or shattered them, and deprived them of a regularized legal status.

Many Church Councils in the earliest Middle Ages had already ordered the separation of Jews and Christians and had required the Jews to wear a badge of shame. This order was renewed by Innocent III in 1215, and also by other popes. The Jews tended to circumvent such edicts or to buy exemption. Sometimes a favorable pope would rescind what a hostile one had ordained. John XXII persecuted the Jews, finally banning the Talmud and ordering it to be publicly burned. But Innocent VII showed them favor, and Martin V, a Roman by birth, did most to protect them. He again granted them the privilege of becoming physicians, and he ordered that all Hebrews in the Church State should contribute to the Carnival levy which had previously been borne by the Jews of Rome alone. But his successor, Eugene IV Condolmieri, a Venetian and like most popes of Venetian origin hostile to the Jews as a trading people, again put them under severe restrictions. He forbade them to associate with Christians, to eat or live with them or to treat them as physicians. He prohibited the Jews from moving about the city and forbade them to build new synagogues and to occupy any public position; the testimony of a Jew against a Christian could not be valid. The Jews had to pay 1,130 gulden into the Capitoline treasury annually, besides meeting other demands and making contributions to the Carnival festivities.

For the Carnival games on the Piazza Navona, at the Testaccio hill, and on the Corso, the custom was gradually established that Jews should be abused for the amusement of the people. Not only did they have to submit to the degradation of having a troop of their elders clothed in jackets or jerkins march before the cavalcade of senators as they led the procession on the Corso, but they themselves were forced to amuse the people with a footrace. It was Paul II, a Venetian, who at the celebration of 1468 as a year of peace first made the Corso races a prime spectacle and made the Jews race in public. To this day it is customary at the festivals in the cities of Italy to race for the so-called *Pallii*, that is, for the prizes of carpets and fine silk stuffs which are awarded to the winner. When Paul gave this festival, races were run on each of the eight days of the Carnival by horses, asses and buffaloes, old men, lads, children, and Jews. Before they were to run, the Jews were richly fed, so as to make the race more difficult for them and at the same time more amusing for the spectators. They ran from the Arch of Domitian to the Church of St. Mark at the end of the Corso at full tilt, amid Rome's taunting shrieks of encouragement and peals of laughter, while the Holy Father stood upon a richly ornamented balcony and laughed heartily. It might seem indeed that the general participation in the races, which embraced Romans—elders, lads, and children—eliminated the degrading aspect; but we must remember that what was a voluntary game to the Romans, in the nature of an Olympic contest, was for the Jews an insult. Anyone who has attended the Corso races at Rome, where horses have now taken the place of the Jews' race, and has seen the raging excitement and heard the shouts and piercing whistles with which the mob urges the rushing beasts on, can easily imagine how in that barbaric age it must have been the gauntlet rather than a race that the driven Jews ran.

Later the people would not be deprived of the Jews' race, and I find it said in Sprenger's *Roma nova* (1667) that the Jews were forced to run nude, wearing only a loin cloth; first, he tells us, the asses ran, then the Jews, then the buffaloes, then Arab horses. For exactly two hundred years the Jews of Rome suffered this revolting indignity, until after repeated petitions they were released from the obligation by papal edict. Clement IX Respigliosi freed them from it in 1668, commuting it into an annual payment of three hundred scudi; instead of the march before the cavalcade of senators they were to render homage in the throne chamber of the Conservatori and to present the Carnival prizes.

On the first Saturday of the Carnival the heads of the Jewish community would appear before the Conservatori on the Capitol as a delegation of Rome's Jewry. They threw themselves down before their seats, and thus kneeling handed them a bouquet of flowers and twenty scudi, with the request that these be used for decorating the balcony on the Piazza del Popolo upon which the Roman senate took their seats. Similarly they went to the Senator and besought his favor in the traditional manner to suffer them to remain in Rome. The Senator set his foot upon their foreheads, bade them rise, and told them according to a traditional formula that Jews were not accepted in Rome, but suffered out of mercy. This humiliation has also disappeared, but even today the Jews come to the Capitol on the first Saturday of the Carnival and deliver their homage and tribute for the accoutrement of the horses, which they are required to provide to commemorate the fact that horses now entertain the people in their stead.

There were other ceremonial acts of homage which the Jews were required to perform in the Middle Ages. When the newly elected pope took possession of the Lateran, a ceremonious deputation of Jews was required to meet him; it is very likely that they had honored the ancient emperors in a similar manner. When a Roman emperor ascended the throne the Hebrews performed sacrifices in the Temple at Jerusalem and offered prayers. In his *Legatio ad Caium* Philo tells us that the Jews had thrice offered sacrifices for Caligula, first when he ascended the throne, again when he fell seriously ill, and finally for his victory in Germany. It is natural to suppose that the Jews in Rome acted similarly, and it is most likely that they were present at the coronations in order to appear before the emperor as suppliants and to pray for such toleration as had been granted them by the Emperor Augustus.

When the popes assumed the position of the emperors only the form, not the substance, of the ceremony was changed. As each new pope received homage, the emissaries of Roman Jewry would appear, a Pentateuch on their shoulder, on the path which the papal triumphal procession was to traverse. According to a dictum of St. Jerome they were regarded as the virtual librarians of the Christian religion, for they had preserved the Old Testament, or rather the Law, in their Ark of the Covenant. When they approached the newly elected pope as suppliants they did so, one may say, partly because their fathers had appeared before the emperors in similar guise, and partly because, hoping for a redeemer and liberator from captivity, they looked to each new pope as a potential liberator from their yoke.

We have reports of each of these ceremonies of homage from the time of Calixtus II, who received such a ceremonial salutation from the Jews in 1119. For each pope they carried a Pentateuch upon their shoulder, for Eugene III as for Alexander III and Gregory IX, and for each they chanted hymns of praise. In his book *Storia de' solenni possessi de' Sommi Pontefici* (1786) Cancellieri provides the best account, drawn from the journals of the papal masters of ceremonies.

The place at which the Jews took their position varied. In the earlier Middle Ages it was the Parione region, one of the oldest and most important quarters of Rome, situated on the left bank at the Bridge of Hadrian; here the Jews awaited the pope on his way to the Lateran. This account is given in the old Latin poem of Cardinal Giacomo Stefaneschi, which describes the inauguration of Boniface VII in 1295:

Ecce, super Tiberim positum de marmore pontem
transierat, provectus equo; turrique relicta
de campo Judaea canens, quae caecula corde est,
occurrit vesana duci Parione sub ipso,
quae Christo gravidam legem plenamque sub umbra
exhibuit Moysi. Veneratus et ille figuram
hanc post terga dedit, cauto sermone locutus.
Ignotus, Judaea, deus, tibi cognitus olim.
Cui quondam populus, nunc hostis; qui deus et rex
obnubi patitur, praesentem temnere mavis,
quem fragilem reputas hominem, sperasque futurum,
et latet ipse deus. . . .*

Even at that early date the exhibition had taken on the forms which were later observed.

* Lo, now mounted upon a horse he had crossed the marble bridge over the Tiber; and when he had left the tower behind him, from the Campus there came to meet the Leader in the midst of Parione chanting Judea, mad and blind in heart. Judea handed over the Law of Moses, pregnant and darkly filled with Christ. He venerated the form of the Law, handed it to those behind him, and uttered prudent speech: Unknown to you, Judea, is the God once known to you. Once you were His people, but now His enemy. He who is God and King has suffered himself to be veiled; you choose to contemn Him though He is present, and regard Him as a fragile mortal, and await one to come; but God himself you do not perceive.

The Jews, chanting hymns of praise, awaited the pope, who rode past in triumphal procession. They offered him a Scroll of the Law, which the pope accepted. He read a few words in it, handed it to those behind him, and said: "We confirm the Law, but condemn the Jewish people and their interpretation." Thereupon he rode on, and the Jews returned to their homes, either crushed to despair or quickened with hope, according as they fearsomely read the expression in the eyes of the pope. They took their stand either behind the Bridge of Hadrian, or as was frequently the case, on the piazza called Monte Giordano. This rubble hill had received its name from Giordano Orsini, a nobleman of the old Roman house of Orsini who had built his palace there; but it was chosen as the site for the Jewish ceremony perhaps because of the name Jordan. There the descendants of Israel stood, holding a Pentateuch handsomely bound in gold and covered with a veil, surrounded by the mocking populace and exposed to all the abuse of scorn and hatred, until the pope appeared and they kneeled and handed him the Law. In course of time the abuse of the Jews on this occasion grew so great that their urgent petitions for relief were granted; in

1484 Innocent VIII Cibo permitted them to appear within the Castle of Sant' Angelo. Burkhard, the master of ceremonies, describes the solemnities as follows:

"As the Pope rode past, he paused near the Castle of Sant' Angelo. The Jews, who had withdrawn to the lowest battlements in a corner of the Castle at the ground level, wearing ceremonial garb and bearing their Law, handed the latter to the Holy Father to pray and do it reverence, addressing him in Hebrew words of approximately this intent: 'All-holiest Father, we Hebrew men petition Your Holiness in the name of our synagogue that we may be found worthy that our Law, delivered to our priest Moses on Mount Sinai by Almighty God, be approved and sanctioned, as other exalted popes, the predecessors of Your Holiness, have approved and sanctioned it.' The Pope answered: 'We sanction the Law, but your belief and your interpretation we condemn, because he of whom you say that he will come has come, our Lord Jesus Christ, as the Church teaches us and preaches.' When the ceremony was completed the Jews withdrew."

If one recalls that the Castle of Sant' Angelo was the tomb of Hadrian, the emperor who had wrought the second destruction of Jerusalem complete and had sold the Jews into slavery, it becomes clear that this spot too had offensive associations in the history of Israel, for the Jews hate the memory of Hadrian like that of Titus.

In 1503 Pius III, because he was ill, made an exception by receiving the Jews in a hall of the Vatican itself. Julius II again received their homage at the tomb of Hadrian. On that occasion they delivered a long address; the Spanish Rabbi Samuel, personal physician to the Pope, spoke with special eloquence. The Pope responded *prout in libello,* that is to say, according to the prescription of the book of ceremonies.

Leo X Medici, whose elevation ceremonies in 1513 were the most brilliant that any pope had had, also received the Jews at the Castle of Sant' Angelo. The scene is described by Paris de Grassis, the master of ceremonies. The Jews stood at the gate of the Castle upon a wooden staging which was covered with gold brocade and silk tapestry and upon which eight white wax tapers were lighted. There they held their Law. When the Pope came riding by upon his white steed, the Jews petitioned for the customary confirmation. He took the open book from their hands, read in it, and then said: "We confirm, but we do not assent" *(confirmamus sed non consentimus).* Then he let the book fall to the ground and continued on his course. This was the last time the ceremony took place at the Castle; thereafter it was abolished, either because of the advanced spirit of the time, or because of some unknown circumstances. Instead, the Hebrews were now required to decorate with costly stuffs the street through which the papal procession moved. At the coronation ceremonies of Gregory XIV (1590) they had to cover the descent of the Capitol and the Arch of Septimius Severus with tapestries. Soon it became the rule that they decorate the Arch of Titus and the road thence to the Colosseum. Thus they had to endure the indignity of ornamenting the triumphal gate they hated because it had been built to honor Jerusalem's destroyer.

This happened at the coronation of all subsequent popes. Upon each occasion the Jews decorated the Arch of Titus, and they were expected to mark the hangings with emblems which related to the pope and with Latin quotations from the Old Testament. The emblems, regularly twenty-five in number, were quite meaningful and employed a fanciful picture language thoroughly oriental in character. For example, there was a representation of a myrtle which distilled its balsam of its own accord, without being cut by a knife, and on it was inscribed the motto, *Beatus rex qui nobilis est* ("Blessed the king who is noble"). There was, furthermore, the pelican, which protects its brood with its own life, bearing the motto, "He hath scattered abroad, he hath given to the needy" (Ps. 112:9.). There was a palm lighted by the sun, with the motto above, "Thou wilt flourish like the righteous palm," and below, "Thy coming in shall be blessed." There was a rhinoceros dipping his horn in a fountain, an open sea shell, the phoenix and a rainbow, a feeding swan, ripe grain, swarms of bees, a mulberry tree, a wreathed harp, a sea with singing sirens and over it the sky with many nightingales flying in it, bearing a line from Isaiah, "Together they sing."

This picture language recalls similar coronation ceremonies of the Sicilian Arabs when they felicitated their lords, the Norman kings. In tears and sorrow the Jews embroidered these hangings of their degradation, and when they had returned from the Arch of Titus to their dirty ghetto they must have purified themselves, with Jeremiad laments and with prayers, from the homage which they had rendered the Vicar of Christ.

One striking feature should be commented on. In the midst of ancient Rome, the mythology of the pagans had pervaded even the Jewish imagination, particularly in that period of the seventeenth and eighteenth centuries that followed Raphael and Leo X and the renewed study of antiquity, when the gods of Olympus again were dominating the world. What can be more amusing and more contradictory than to see this tendency reflected even by the Jews of Rome, and especially in the eighteenth century, the golden age of the baroque Parnassus! Their emblems too become mythologic, their poems of homage speak of Apollo and the Muses, and in the intermingling of classical and Old Testament elements the confusion of the imagination becomes truly comical and the inconsistency all the greater if one reflects that it is to a pope that these poems and emblems are dedicated by the people of Israel. Most of the mythologic emblems are found in the Jews' offerings to Pius VI and Pius VII. There was Hercules, gold chains issuing from his mouth with which to draw the people, and underneath a verse of Scripture, "The lips of the righteous know what is acceptable" (Prov. 10:32). There was Mount Parnassus on one side and on the other a platform covered with tapestry upon which horses and mules were feeding on grain, and a motto from Job, "By draft beasts he teacheth us." One can imagine no more baroque combination than Parnassus, a mule, and Job. There was Juno with a lily, Atlas bearing the world upon his shoulders, Minerva with the olive branch, a temple containing Mercury and the Three Graces, and underneath the legend, "No good thing will He withhold from them that walk uprightly" (Ps. 84:12). Of all the gods of mythology, Mercury, the patron of merchants and brokers, the Rothschild of the Olympians, must have been the classical figure most intelligible to the ghetto The emblems of this poor people were always more or less related to one and the same idea, money and again money; hence Amalthea's cornucopias, from which gold coins, wine, and bread poured forth, were especial favorites.

To Pope Pius VII Chiaramonti the Jews presented all their emblems and mottoes bound in a costly little book. The presentation was made by Rabbi Leone di Leone d'Ebron in Venice, wearing a long beard, caftan, and oriental turban. The superscription of the poem of dedication, in Latin elegiacs, read as follows:

PIO SEPTIMO P.O.M.
QUA DIE IMPERII GUBERNACULA SOLEMNITER SUSCIPIT
QUOD BONUM FELIX FAUSTUMQUE SIT
FESTIVISSIMA HEBRAEORUM UNIVERSITAS D.D.D.

It was not for nothing, one sees, that Rome's classical Jews had dwelt near the Porticus of Roman Octavia. The poem itself began in the typically Jewish manner with a lament, and then proceeded to deal with Apollo and the Pope himself:

O me si cithara plectroque iuvaret Apollo,
   concinerem summi maxima regna Pii,
meque peregrinis audiret versibus uti,
   quidquid habet tellus, quidquid et axis habet.
Principis astra super ferrem clarissima facta,
   quis comes it recti non temerandus amor:
quippe suis, velut illa polo, fulgoribus umbras
   dimovet, e vultu quos radiante iacit.
Ut pro me Pindi veniant et culmine Musae
   quas cecinit vatum fabula Graeca deas.
Hae resona fundant solemnia carmina voce,
   tympana pulsantes, sistra lyrasque manu,
hae Themidis celebrent servantem iura decorae,
   qua duce subiectis imperat agminibus:
candoremque sinus dantis cum pace salutem,
   viribus ingenii, pondere consilii.
Magnanimis nitet ille notis, prudentibus aeque,
   ne summum videat gloria tanta diem!
Culmina Gregorius nutu quae celsa creavit,
   sospitet, omnigenis condecoretque bonis.
Edat, ut arbor aquae prope rivos consita, fructus,
   et diadema suum vinciat usque caput.

Hic niteat solusque ferax sit dactylus ipsi:
adspiciat laetos ire, redire dies.

Gaudeat urbs, precibus nunquam non acribus instet,
ut sibi sint Pacis munera iuncta Piae.*

For Gregory XVI the Jews commissioned Pietro Paoletti, a painter of Belluno, because Gregory was a native of that town, to produce a richly bound book containing emblems and poems. The Pope presented it to the chapter of the cathedral

---

* Oh that Apollo with lyre and plectrum may assist me, so that I may sing of the great dominion of sublime Pius, and that whatever earth holds, whatever the vault of heaven, may hear me as I utter alien verses. Let me bear aloft, higher than the stars, the famous deeds of our prince, which undefiled love of righteousness attends as comrade. Nay, he dispels the shades, as do the stars in heaven, by his own shining rays, which he casts forth from his radiant countenance. May the Muses come to my aid from the heights of Pindus, the Muses whom the Greeks fabled to be the goddesses of bards. May they pour forth their solemn strains with sounding voice, their hands striking tympana, tambourine, and lyre. May they celebrate the guardian of the law of seemly Themis, by whose guidance he bears sway over subject hordes; may they celebrate the pure spirit of one who by the strength of his genius and the weight of his counsel vouchsafes safety with peace. He shines forth by his celebrated magnanimity, and by his prudence withal: may glory so great never see its final day! May Gregory preserve in safety the lofty heights which he has created by his nod, and may he enhance them with all manner of good. May he give forth fruit like a tree planted by streams of water, and may the diadem long wreathe his brow. Here may he shine in splendor, and for him alone may my dactyls be fertile. May he behold joyous days come and return. May the City rejoice, and may it offer ever earnest prayers that the gifts of Pius' peace remain bound up with its own.

of his native city as a mark of esteem. A similar book was presented to Pius IX, the present incumbent. The rabbi of Rome, who is very skilful in writing, as the Hebrews assured me, inscribed it with artistic emblems and quotations from Scripture. Its ornamentation and binding were so elegant that it was said to have cost five hundred scudi.

Such were the Jewish ceremonies, characterized by local and Roman coloring, which attended upon the inauguration of the popes. But the same sort of thing took place under other conditions also. In Corfu, we read in Moroni's *Dizinario,* the Jews felicitated the newly elected archbishop with great pomp. When Francesco Maria Fenzi made his entry into Corfu in 1780 the Jews staged an extraordinary spectacle. The procession was opened by a Jew in Italian dress carrying a general's staff. He was followed by three Jews with longer staves, representing the three patriarchs. Then came twelve young men in Italian dress, each with a silver apple in his hand, representing the twelve tribes. Behind them came ten other young men with the *tallit* over their shoulders, representing the ten sage rabbis who were the keepers of the Mosaic Law at the time of Caesar. Then followed eleven young men with flowers in their hands, dressed as the brothers of Joseph, and represented as going to Pharaoh, together with their four servants. Then eight men with vessels and palms represented the eight guardians of the rite of circumcision. Then twenty-four, double the number of the tribes, with silver implements and basins and gloves in hand, representing the flower of Israel. There followed a train of forty-eight Jews with fur caps, and after them six singers, chanting psalms from books. Then four Jews with large wigs and staves, and after them fifteen young men with Urim and Tummim on their breasts, then a train with fruits and palms, and after them singers once more. Then the four High Priests, Moses, Aaron, David, and Solomon, followed by Levites. Behind them marched the three from the fiery furnace. The procession was closed by the hoary chief rabbi, who wearing a long white robe looked like fasting incarnate, and at his side marched two elders holding basins filled with flower petals. Behind them the Pentateuch was carried, hung about with bells, apples, crowns, and other decorations of silver, under a white canopy borne by four sturdy Jews. At six points in the city the Pentateuch was opened, whereat the Jewish populace uttered a loud cry, and scattered flowers out of the basins over the Law. Those that fell to the earth were snatched up by Jewish women and kept in their bosoms as a sacred keepsake. The parade itself had four supervisors, in memory of the four captivities of Egypt, Babylon, Rome, and the present. On an elegantly decorated loge near the cathedral, the Archbishop was finally welcomed by sixteen Jews. The prelate stood erect with miter and crosier, and when a Jew covered himself, drawing his *tallit* over his head, and pronounced a complimentary address, the Archbishop responded in kind.

It is clear that so magnificent a parade of a genuinely national Jewish character might well take place in Corfu, but could never happen in Rome. There, where Christianity or its cult appeared essentially in the form of the procession, a national Hebrew display would have shown the people that the greater part of Catholic pomp, or what was not ancient pagan or medieval Christian, was only a reflection of ancient Jewish processions. But that was not the reason why the Jews in Rome did not stage such affairs, and it is idle to speak of such considerations. The street lads of Rome would have stoned a public parade of a Mosaic character, and it would have been drowned in the sea of public mockery. Also the Jews of Rome were probably careful to make no display of gold and silver, and when they appeared at the papal processions they put on, for appearance' sake, an air of poverty and humble neediness, anxiety and trembling and pathetic servility.

We turn now to the fate of the Jews under the successors of that Paul II who first required the Jews to race at the Carnival. Sometimes the pressure was severe and sometimes it relaxed, as for example, under the Roman Pope Paul III Farnese; their fate was finally fixed in the reign of Paul IV. This Neapolitan of the fanatic and violent house of Caraffa, a Theatine and an Inquisitor, founder of the torture chambers and of the censorial office in Rome, a pitiless reformer of iron determination, had scarcely ascended the papal throne when he issued in 1555 the bull *Cum nimis absurdum* which regulated the position of Roman Jewry. He rescinded all former privileges of the Hebrews; he forbade their physicians to treat Christians, and forbade Jews to engage in any trade or handicraft or to purchase real property. He increased their tribute and imposts, and forbade them to associate with Christians. He even forbade the use of the title 'Don,' which some Jews following the Spanish and Portuguese custom employed. In order to make their separation from the Christians complete he ordered that they must not be seen outside the ghetto without wearing a yellow hat and yellow veil, the former for men and the latter for women, "for," says the bull, "it is absurd and improper that the Jews who have fallen into eternal servitude by their own guilt should presume, under the pretext that Christian charity has taken them up, to make so bold as to live intermingled with Christians, to wear no distinguishing mark, to employ Christian servants, even to purchase houses."

Finally Paul IV set up the ghetto, or Jews' enclosure. Previous to his time the Jews were at liberty, though the privilege was not specified, to live anywhere in Rome. Naturally they seldom chose to live in the middle of the city or scattered among the Christians who hated them, but kept together in Trastevere and on the riverbank up to the Bridge of Hadrian. Now the Pope, following Venetian usage, assigned them a sharply secluded quarter which embraced a few narrow streets immediately on the Tiber and extended from the Quattro Capi Bridge to the modern Piazza of Tears. Walls or gates shut this Jewish quarter in. At first it was called *vicus Judaeorum;*

then the name ghetto came into use. This name appears to have no relation to the Venetian appellation *Giudecca* and apparently is formed from the talmudic word *get,* which signifies separation.* It was on July 26, 1556, that the Jews of Rome moved into this ghetto, sobbing and sighing like their ancestors, for that they were being led into captivity.

Thus Paul IV Caraffa proved to be a cruel Pharaoh to the Jews of Rome, exposing them to all the evils which inevitably arose from want of space and the low situation of the houses along the riverbank. These evils included pestilence and malaria and a host of Egyptian plagues whose horrors truly beggar description. When Caraffa died in 1559 and the Roman populace rose to vent its rage against him, plundering the house of the Inquisition, and storming Minerva, the monastery of the Dominicans, one could see the Jews also, timorous people who had not even participated in the revolutions at the time of Cola di Rienzo, issue from their corral and hurl curses upon the memory of Paul IV. One Jew even ventured to set the yellow hat of shame upon the statue of the Pope on the Capitol; the populace

* [The talmudic *get* simply means 'document,' though it did come to denote 'bill of divorce'; the derivation offered in the text is incorrect.—*Tr.*]

laughed, broke the monument to fragments, and dragged the head with its papal crown through the mud. The fate which befell the Jews of Rome after the introduction of the new heresy tribunals of the Inquisition is familiar to those who are acquainted with the history of the period. Many Jews were burnt on the Piazza of Minerva or the Campo dei Fiori where the autos-da-fé were held. It was the fearful time when Giordano Bruno too was burnt alive.

Imprisoned in the ghetto, Jews became subject to outside owners. For the houses of the quarter belonged to Romans; some respected families had lived there, as for example the Boccapaduli. When they removed they remained landlords, and the Jews tenants. But because they were to be limited to the quarter forever they had to establish a permanent rental arrangement, for otherwise they were liable to two mischiefs: homelessness, if it should occur to the landlord to give his Hebrew tenant notice; and intolerable indebtedness or inability to pay if it occurred to him to raise the rental. So a law was instituted which ordained that the Romans should retain title to the dwellings rented to Jews, but that the leasehold of the Jews should be hereditary. The owner might never force the Jewish tenant to vacate, as long as he paid his rental properly, and the rental might never be raised; furthermore the Jew might alter or enlarge his house at will. This law was (and is, for it still exists) called *jus gazaga;* it gave the Jew hereditary possession of his lease, which he might then transfer to relatives or others. Even today the ownership of a *jus gazaga* or hereditary lease is regarded as a most precious possession; and enviable is the lot of the Jewish maiden who can bring her bridegroom such a document as dowry. And so this beneficial law gave the Jew a roof which he might in a sense call his own.

The bull of Paul IV was confirmed by Pius V Ghislieri in 1566. This Pope issued severe ordinances against Jews wandering about the city; they were required to be within the ghetto at nightfall. For after Ave Maria the gates of the enclosure were inexorably shut, and anyone caught outside was liable to severe penalty if he was unable to bribe the watchmen with money. In 1569 the same Pope forbade the Jews residence in the cities of the Church State other than Rome and Ancona; previously they had been tolerated in Benevento and Avignon also.

But hardly had the edict been issued when Sixtus V rescinded it and so caused a glimmer of hope and humanity to illuminate the misery of the ghetto. In general the change of popes altered all conditions in Rome, as in a *tombola* or lottery wheel. Sixtus V, a man of humane sentiment, happy, clever, the Christian restorer of Rome whose name is recalled in almost every street and every building, took pity on the people of Israel. In 1586 he issued the bull *Christiana pietas infelicem Hebraeorum statum commiserans,* wherein he reinstated the former privileges of the Jews. He granted them liberty to live in the Roman territory, that is, in walled places, cities, and fortresses. He permitted them to engage in any trade or business except traffic in wine, grain, and meat. He allowed them free intercourse with Christians, so that they might even make use of Christian facilities without, however, keeping Christian servants. He was concerned for greater comfort in their dwellings, he generously allowed them as many schools and synagogues as they required, and he allowed the establishment of Hebrew libraries. He prohibited the bringing of Jews before the court on their holy days, he abolished the Jews' badge, he forbade Jewish children to be baptized under coercion, and traveling Jews to be burdened with extraordinary levies. He moderated the tribute and reduced the levy to little beyond the requirement for the expenses of the Carnival *Pallii*. Thus Sixtus gave the world an example of a Christian pope and made his memory blessed for all time; what he did for the Jews out of his own magnanimous spirit is an enduring ornament to his name.

Here then the Hebrews made one lucky strike in the *tombola;* but because its nature was like that of a lottery, the wheel might suddenly turn. And so it came to pass. A few years after Sixtus V's death, Clement VIII Aldobrandini withdrew all the ordinances relating to Jews, renewed Caraffa's edict, and so thrust the Jews back into despair. Their misery not only continued through the seventeenth century, but was augmented in the eighteenth by the edicts of Clement XI and Innocent XIII. The latter forbade the Jews all business except trade in old cloth and rags and old iron, called *stracci ferracci.* It was only in 1740 that Benedict XIV Lambertini permitted them trade in new textiles also, which Jews pursue diligently at this day. Until this time they could be seen hawking old clothes in the streets and crying "Hep!"—the call by which they announced their presence and invited purchasers of their rubbish.

The sixteenth and seventeenth centuries, during which the Medici granted the Jews of Tuscany such great liberty, was perhaps the most oppressive period which the people of the Roman ghetto experienced. In a Roman book of 1677, *Stato vero degli Ebrei in Roma, Stamperia del Varese,* I find it reported that the Jewish population amounted to 4,500, among whom were two hundred prosperous families. The author states that in the sixteenth century the ghetto was required to pay 4,861 scudi in tribute, whereas in the seventeeth century the sum had fallen to 3,207 scudi. Although this book is extremely hostile to the Jews, I should not venture to dismiss it all as lies. The author remarks that despite the complaints which the Jews were constantly drawing up, the ghetto was in fact rich, that after payment of all dues 19,470 scudi were set aside every five years, and that the ghetto possessed a fortune of a million scudi. Without doubt there were rich Jews in Rome at the time. Along with the fences, thieves' accomplices, and necromancers of the ghetto, there was the usurer, rogue of rogues, who heaped interest upon interest. No pope was able to suppress this Jewish banking business. The indebted nobles protected the Jews, and while the ghetto was covered with scorn, the Roman noble and cardinal, even the pope himself, received the yellow-hatted usurer in his palace. The author of the book declares that the Jews had exacted 235,000 scudi from the Christians in usury, and that no evening passed without at least eight hundred scudi being drawn from Christian purses through the ghetto gates into Jewish houses. That crafty people knew all the arts of dishonest gain; and their usury must have nourished the hatred of the Christians. John of Capistrano once offered Eugene IV a fleet for transporting the Jews bag and baggage across the sea. "Now that he is dead," says the justly embittered author, "it is to be wondered that he does not send Pope Clement IX a fleet from heaven so as to rid Rome of all these thieves." The interest rate of the Jewish Rothschilds at the time was 18 per cent. Until today Jewish money has remained an avenging power; even today the ghetto lends money at interest. Here everything turns upon money and profit, and how could it be otherwise? As I was walking through a street of the ghetto one day a wretched Jewess who was sewing on rags called to me, "Sir, what do you require?" To test the woman's presence of mind I turned to her suddenly and said, "Five millions." "Good," she replied as quickly, "four for me and one for you." Yes, Israel cannot deny itself.

In the eighteenth century it was a strict requirement that Jews attend Christian conversionist sermons on stated days. As early as 1572 Gregory XIII had issued an ordinance that they be required to attend one such sermon each week. It was a Jew who introduced this usage, a convert, naturally, Andreas by name, who with the dog's spirit of a convert pressed Pope Gregory to issue the decree. On the Sabbath, then, police catchpolls were to be seen entering the ghetto and whipping the Jews to church, men, women, and children, if they were over twelve years old. It was required that at least a hundred men and fifty women, the number later being raised to three hundred, attend the sermon. At the door of the church a watchman counted those that entered. In the church itself catchpolls observed the attentiveness of those present, and if a Jew seemed not to participate or to doze he was aroused by strokes of the whip and blows. The sermon was given by a Dominican, the all-holiest was taken from the altar. He spoke on such texts of the Old Testament as the Jews had heard read or interpreted that day in their synagogue, so that the Catholic interpretation should follow immediately upon the Jewish and the Hebrew thus be in position to recognize Christian truth. At first the sermons were given in San Benedetto alla Regola, later in that Church of Sant' Angelo in Pescaria from which Cola di Rienzo once delivered his inspired addresses to the Romans.

Let us turn our glance for a moment to this small church built into the dark Porticus of Octavia, the church of the fishmonger angel. It arouses memories of one of the most remarkable men of the Roman Middle Ages. Cola was born in 1313 in the *rione* of Regola, that is, near the Jewish quarter. As Rienzo's *Vita* tells us, his house was situated at the river's edge between the mills on the road leading to Regola, behind San Tomasso under the Jews' Temple *(sotto lo tempio de li Judei)*. There his father Lorenzo kept an inn and his mother Maddalena earned their support by washing and carrying water. Thus his house was near the Church of Sant' Angelo in Pescaria, and it was here that he had the remarkable allegorical picture painted upon the outer wall. The picture showed kings and men of the people burning in a fire, and also a matron who was half consumed, and on the right a church from which a white-robed angel came, naked sword in hand, while with his left hand he drew the matron out of the fire. On the summit of the clock tower stood St. Peter and St. Paul and they said, "Angel, angel, help our inn-mother" *(Agnilo, agnilo:*

succuri a l'albergatrice nostra). Besides, many falcons (barons) could be seen falling from the sky into the fire, and a beautiful white dove carrying a myrtle wreath in its beak and giving it to a small bird (Rienzo), who chased the falcons out of the sky and then set the myrtle wreath upon the head of the matron. Underneath was the legend: "I see the time of the great judgment; do thou await that time." This was the picture which Cola had caused to be painted. The *Vita* calls the church that of the Angel Fishmonger *(de santo Agnilo Pescivennolo),* because even then fish were sold in the Porticus of Octavia. Here the Jews must have streamed to observe the painting, but we do not hear that they participated in the insurrection, and only after Rienzo's death did they actively, and in a strange way tread the stage of this tragedy. It was they who performed the last rites for the body of the tribune of the people. When he was murdered on the Capitol, the people dragged his mangled corpse to the Piazza San Marcello where he was hanged by the feet. There he remained for two days, a target for the stones of street boys, until on the third day Jugurta and Sciarretta Colonna ordered that the body be brought to the mausoleum of Augustus. Here, as the biography states, all the Jews assembled in great number, not one remaining behind, and they built a fire of dry thistles, and in it cast the corpse; it was fat and because of its great fatness burnt easily *(ardeva volentieri)*. There stood the Jews, very busily and assiduously piling thistles into the heap of fire. Thus the corpse was rendered dust, no shred of it remaining. It is not to be thought that it was loyalty which moved the Jews to render Cola this service, which the Roman people regarded as a profound insult. It was rather that the Jews wished to flatter the Colonnas. Rienzo's strict regime, which had introduced a new order into all things, could hardly be longed for by those who fished in troubled waters and enriched themselves by receiving stolen goods and usury.

But let us come back to the conversionist sermons. They were later given only five times annually, and the custom was on the verge of disappearing when Leo XII Genga (1823-1829) revived it. Today this barbarity too has disappeared; it was abolished, I have been told, in the first year of the liberal reign of Pius IX.

The Jew who was converted to Christianity naturally profited by liberation from the ghetto; he received civic rights and all the human rights therein entailed. It happened not infrequently that Jews from the ghetto were baptized; they then became, as is in the character of converts, more zealous proselytizers than their converters. Thus on a church opposite the ghetto, at the Bridge of Quattro Capi, on whose façade the Crucifixion is painted, one may read the second verse of the sixty-fifth chapter of Isaiah inscribed in Hebrew and Latin characters: "I have spread out My hands all the day unto a rebellious people, that walk in a way that is not good, after their own thoughts." This is an admonition which a converted Jew has caused to be inscribed there in order to flatter his new faith. According to the medieval custom, Jews who were baptized received the names of their godfathers, and since they sought godfathers among the most respected houses of Rome it happened that Jews smuggled themselves into the oldest families of Roman aristocracy. Many a baptized Jew thenceforward called himself by the name of the nobleman who had been his godfather, and so there were Jewish Colonna, Jewish Massinni, Jewish Orsini; indeed it is conjectured in Rome today that many a proud princely Roman family, after it had died out, was carried forward by Jews from Trastevere.

Today when the old abuses have disappeared from the light of day, the old traditional public rite of a solemn baptism of Jews and Turks has nevertheless been retained as a form. It takes place annually on the eve of Easter Sunday in the baptistery of the Lateran, and it is said that this performance must be carried out at all costs, even if it becomes necessary in the event that no convert is available to bring a Jew or a Turk from abroad. In 1853 a Jewess was baptized before a large gathering and with most solemn ceremonies. This daughter of Judah, not fair as Rebecca but of exquisite ugliness, stood at the baptismal font swathed in a white veil, with a burning taper, the symbol of illumination, in her hand, and after her head and the nape of her neck were thoroughly anointed and she had received the initiation of water in that font of Constantine in which Cola di Rienzo had once bathed in rose water, she was led back to the Lateran in procession. The cardinal who had baptized her blessed her before the altar, and when the ceremony was finished, pointing to the baptized woman he expressed his joy to the people that so sublime and divine a miracle had been consummated, that a person who but a moment ago was possessed of demons, and a prey of hell, had suddenly been clothed in the pure innocence of a child and in the pure light of God. Earlier expressions were stronger. In his book

Stuore (Venice, 1662) the Jesuit Stephan Menochio declares that Jews' bodies stink but that they lose their stench immediately after baptism. Naively he tells us that even the Emperor Marcus Aurelius had complained of the stench of the Jews. This was an accepted fact, and the Agarenes had caused themselves to be baptized in order to be rid of their evil, dog-like smell.

Leo XII, of whom we know that he was not favorably disposed to the Jews, nevertheless gave them the right to acquire houses if they already possessed the *jus gazaga*. He also enlarged the compass of the ghetto by adding the Via Reginella and a portion of the Pescaria, so that it now had eight gates which were watched and kept locked at night. During the French rule of Rome the ghetto bars were removed, as one might easily surmise, and the Jews were allowed to live anywhere in the city and pursue trades. But in 1814 Pius VII closed the ghetto anew, and it remained in its old state until the reign of the present Pope. It is to the honor of Pius IX that he, more humane and liberal than his predecessors, tore down the bars of the ghetto. This happened, as Jews have expressly informed me, not as a result of the latest revolution in Rome, but a year before, for public opinion and the reforming temper of the Pope demanded this concession to the moral sensibilities of the century. Walls and gates which had barred the ghetto fell. The change in policy brought other desirable results: Jews were permitted to reside anywhere in Rome and they acquired the right to engage in trades and handicrafts. Thus as a forced enclosure the ghetto is abolished, but it continues in fact as the dreariest quarter in Rome, a corner of filth and poverty. It is not easy for the Jew to make use of his right to remove to the center of the city because, as I have been told, what the law now permits is made endlessly difficult if not quite impossible by ineradicable prejudice. As I was standing at the fountain of Navona one day (it was a Saturday) a number of Jewish women in holiday attire came up and looked at the fountain. A Roman woman regarded them with contempt and then said to me, "Look, look, now they are like Christians."

Thus the political reforms of 1847 denoted the end of that slavery which the Jews of Rome had endured for so many centuries. We may at the least hope that the power of public opinion will prove stronger than any capricious prejudice, if it should in the future be renewed, and that the slight liberties which the Jews have now attained will be extended, so that they may be given unqualified participation in all the advantages of culture and civilization. The prospects are indeed remote, but they have drawn nearer.

At present the total population of the ghetto is reckoned at 3,800, a disproportionately large number considered in relation to its small area, which amounts to less than a fifth of the area of any town of three thousand persons. The entire Jewry (*Università degli Ebrei*) is subject to the Congregation of the Inquisition, and its special magistracy for all civil and criminal cases is the cardinal-vicariate. The tribunal which sits in judgment consists of the Cardinal Vicar, the *Prelato Vicegerente,* the *Prelato Luogotenente Civile,* and the *Luogotenente Criminale.* Police matters are in the hands of the local magistracy of the president of the Region of Sant' Angelo and Campitelli. The Jewish community itself has the right to regulate its internal order by three so-called *Fattori del Ghetto,* who are elected for a half year. These officials are in charge of traffic, light, and water supply; they apportion taxes according to wealth of the individual, and provide for care of the sick, distribution of alms, and the like. Altogether the annual payments of the ghetto to the state and to various religious corporations amount to some 13,000 francs

We have brought the history of the Jews of Rome to an end. We shall now consider the Roman ghetto in its present state as we have come to know it from personal observation.

The ghetto is reached either from the city, by way of the Theater of Marcellus and the Porticus of Octavia through Via Savelli, or from Trastevere, by way of the Tiber island and the Bridge of Quattro Capi. This bridge affords a most striking view of ancient and medieval Rome, a picture so strange and enchanting as can hardly be paralleled in this city of memories. On one side is colorful Trastevere, with its old architecture and broken towers; along the river are the arches of the Ponte Rotto and beyond are the pretty temple of Vesta, the old tower of Santa Maria in Cosmedin, the gigantic ruins of the imperial palaces with their black cypresses on the Palatine, and in the distance the peaks of the Alban hills; but directly ahead are the ghetto houses in a row, tower-like masses of bizarre design, with numerous flowerpots in the windows and countless household utensils hanging on the walls. The rows ascend from the river's edge, and its dismal billows wash against the walls. It is only a few steps from the bridge to the ghetto, whose level is extremely low. When I first visited it the Tiber had overflowed its banks and its yellow flood streamed through the Fiumara, the lowest of the ghetto streets, the foundations of whose houses serve as a quay to hold the river in its course. The flood reached as far up as the Porticus of Octavia, and water covered the lower rooms of the houses at the bottom. What a melancholy spectacle to see the wretched Jews' quarter sunk in the dreary inundation of the Tiber! Each year Israel in Rome has to undergo a new Deluge, and like Noah's Ark the ghetto is tossed on the waves with man and beast. When the Tiber, swollen with mountain snow and torrents of rain, and driven back by the west wind from the sea, goes into flood misery is multiplied. Those who live beneath take refuge in the upper floors, which are intolerably crowded and tainted by pestilential atmosphere. The stoppage of food supply and of work increase the misfortune, and the flood ruins everything that cannot be removed. I was shown the high-water mark of the ghetto inundation of 1846; on that occasion water filled all lower floor rooms to their ceilings. Last fall and this spring the Tiber flooded for only a short period, but even this minor calamity seemed to me bad enough, and its consequences, because of the great crowding and poverty, very sad. Nevertheless the mortality rate in the ghetto during the cholera year of 1837 seems to have been slight; gauged by the number of Jewish tombstones their dead were very few. These white stones with their inscriptions stand isolated, clinging to one another like a pitiful group of exiles, on a classical site, in a corner of the Circus Maximus, surrounded by wild grass and poisonous blooms of cowbane. Where Tarquinius Priscus had built Rome's first racecourse the Jewish cemetery, called *Orto degli Ebrei,* is now situated. So do times change.

Is there not a certain wonderful irony in the fact that a locale is impressed upon the physiognomy of people and things, so that they are suffused with it as with a characteristic atmosphere? I have noticed this principle too often not to mention it. The physiognomy of the ghetto environment struck me as penetrating the atmosphere with gloomy imaginings. I do not mean that Porticus of Octavia associated with Jewish history which now lies fallen in filth, its ruined and blackened arches gaping upon the stinking Pescaria, that crowded and dark fish market where the Jews' fasting fare is laid out on stone slabs; nor do I mean the blackened remains of the Theater of Marcellus in whose ruins the

Savelli, once fearsome robber knights in the land, built their palace and where many an unfortunate ended his days in a dungeon; nor yet the memories of Cola di Rienzo. Let us read the names on the piazza which lies hard by the Jews' Square. By the Church of Santa Maria del Pianto it is the Place of Tears, a suitable name for taking one to the Jeremiad people in the ghetto quarter, for whom Lamentations is a national trait; and never has a people wept more than these Jews here in Rome. On the Place of Tears there stands an old palace between two churches. The inscription on one states that it is dedicated to Mary of Sorrows; the other bears the gruesome name of its builder, Francesco Cenci. The palace is that of the Cenci; here the beholder is struck with horror when he recalls the beautiful Beatrice Cenci, Francesco's unhappy daughter, the murderess of a monstrous father. The palace looks across the Jews' Square directly at the synagogue, in which on festal days the Psalms and Lamentations of the Hebrews are to be heard.

In this palace dwells the painter Overbeck; again, what marvelous irony. I had to smile when I entered the atelier; quiet people enter here as quietly as if it were a sanctuary, and a pale man with parted, long hair, a man amiable, gentle, hardly audible, not really speaking but rather breathing forth soft words, explains the sacred pictures on the easels. These too are quiet and without tone: a sleeping Joseph in the arms of the Savior, a shadowy sorrowing Madonna, a Christ soaring above his persecutors and treading upon airy clouds, winged heads of infant angels without bodies—disembodied people, disembodied art, speech without words, pictures without color, the Madonna Dolorosa, the Passion on the wall, the tragedy of the Cenci. Yonder the flooded ghetto, here the holy Mary of Sorrows, and in the midst of all the Beato Angelico of modern painting. The point is that in this palace of the Cenci, a few steps from the ghetto and from the Jews' synagogue, Overbeck lives and paints his Christian pictures as though under the inspiration of the spirit of Jehovah and of the prophets. Here side by side, as they should be, are the Old Testament and the New; and as I stand between the palace of the Cenci and the synagogue of the Jews, it always seems to me as if both lie open before me, the Old Covenant and the New, Judaism and Christianity.

Before 1847 a high wall still separated the Place of the Cenci from the Jews' Square which is also called Piazza delle Scuole. Here was the principal gate of the ghetto; wall and gate are now torn down, and part of their rubble still lies scattered about. If we now enter the streets of the ghetto itself we find Israel before its booths, buried in restless toil and distress. They sit in their doorways or outdoors on the street which affords scarcely more light than their damp and dismal rooms, and tend their ragged merchandise or industriously patch and sew. The chaos of patching and mending (called *cenci* in Italian) is indescribable. All the world seems to lie about, transformed into Jewish trash, tattered and torn, in countless rags and scraps. Pieces of junk of every kind and color are heaped high before the doors: scraps of golden fringe, pieces of silk brocade, rags of velvet, patches of red, scraps of blue, orange, yellow, black, white, old, torn, threadbare, badly worn scraps and tatters. I have never seen the like. The Jews might patch all creation with it and make the whole world as varicolored as a harlequin. They sit before it and wallow in the sea of patches as if they were searching for a treasure or at least a sunken piece of gold brocade. For they are as much researchers in Roman antiquity as are those in Rome who grovel through rubble in order to bring to the light of day the stump of a column, a fragment of a relief, an old inscription, a coin, or similar plunder. The Hebrew Winckelmann in the ghetto exposes his rags for sale with a certain pride like that of the dealer in marble fragments. The latter swaggers with a piece of *giallo antico,* and the Jew can rival him with an excellent scrap of yellow satin; porphyry?—here is an excellently patterned scrap of crimson damask; *verde antico?*—here is a beautiful green velvet patch of exquisite antiquity. And so there is neither jasper nor alabaster, neither black and white marble nor breccia, for which the antiquarian of the ghetto cannot provide matching rarities. The history of all fashion from Herod the Great to the inventor of the paletot, and all costumes of the noble as of the bourgeois world, can be critically constructed by ingenious hypotheses on the basis of these rags. Many scraps are apparently historical and may once have been worn by Romulus, Scipio Africanus, Hannibal, or Cornelia, by Charlemagne, Pericles, Cleopatra, Barbarossa, by Gregory VII, Columbus, or similar worthies.

The daughters of Zion sit upon these rags and stitch anything that can be stitched. They have a reputation for great art in patching, darning, and piecing, and it is said that no rent in any sort of drapery or fabric can be so fearful that these Arachnes cannot make it invisible and untraceable. This trade is carried on mostly in the Fiumara, the nethermost street hard by the river, and in the corner alleys, of which one is called delle Azzimelle, which means unleavened bread. It was frequently with painful sympathy that I looked upon them, pale and exhausted and stooped, as they diligently plied their needles, men as well as women, girls and children. Misery stared from their ruffled hair and lamented from their sallow faces. No facial beauty recalled Rachel and Leah or Miriam. Occasionally one encountered a black, sunken, gleaming eye looking up from needle and rags, as if to say: "Gone is from the daughter of Zion all her splendour. She that was great among the nations, and princess among the provinces, how is she become tributary! She weepeth sore in the night, and her tears are on her cheeks. She hath none to comfort her among all her lovers; all her friends have dealt treacherously with her, they are become her enemies. Judah is gone into exile because of affliction, and because of great servitude; she dwelleth among the nations, she findeth no rest. All her pursuers entreat her ill. How hath the Lord covered with a cloud the daughter of Zion in His anger!"

But it is not the purpose of these pages to depict the mysteries of the ghetto's wretchedness or to gape at the customs of these needy people in their overcrowded rooms. In the great cities of the earth and among the civilized nations of Europe one may find equal if not greater wretchedness. Nor must it be thought that the ghetto of Rome, as far as streets and houses are concerned, is in itself more miserable than similar haunts of poverty in many other cities of the world. I prefer to say that the Jews of Rome are rich in humanity to one another, that the prosperous cheerfully help the poor, that the self-sacrificing solidarity of the family, which is Israel's enduring heritage, can nowhere show itself so strong and so beneficent as here, and that it continues true that these sober and industrious people are seldom punished for crime. What most horrifies the spectator in the ghetto is the narrowness and filth of these tortuous streets and alleys and the narrow houses which reach high above them. In them Jewish families live as in a Roman columbarium, stacked one over the other in rows. It is remarkable that such crowding should take place in Rome, a city extending over a broad plain and itself characterized by spreading spaciousness, by an architecture of large and lofty dimensions, and by palaces in which one might comfortably house half the Jewish city of the ghetto. In majestic halls the stone population of statues dwell amidst cool fountains. The marble remains of antiquity, down to the slightest fragment, are royally housed; the only living remains of ancient Rome, human beings with long-enduring hearts, live in wretched filth.

More fortunate are those Jews who inhabit the upper portion of the ghetto, particularly the Via Rua. This broad street with its more habitable houses is virtually the Corso of the Jewish quarter; for also under equal political conditions, and even in slavery, men will find a way to assert the right to inequality. In the Via Rua there live Jews who hold the best *gazaga* documents in their pockets and who themselves own property and are well off. Here one finds textile shops stocked with wares ranging from the coarsest to the daintiest. There are also some prosperous Jews; if they grow wealthy, I am told, they are eager to go to Tuscany. It is striking that genuinely Jewish names are nowhere to be read. The Jews of Rome mostly call themselves after Italian cities, like Astrubale, Volterra, Samuele Fiano, Pontecorvo, Gonzaga; and it is amusing to find them bearing these proud and princely-sounding names. Their language too is Roman, and only rarely have I heard Jews speaking Hebrew among themselves. Their dress is no different from that of the Roman people, and even at their festivals I have noticed not a single oriental costume.

A festival in the ghetto—bordering on the ironical if one reflects on the history and status of the Jewish community. Such a spectacle should be particularly attractive in Rome, where one festival treads upon the heels of another, and where one day, resplendent with display, only leads the wearied foreigner to another awaiting his attention. While these magnificent festival processions move through the streets of Rome, all the world enjoying them with gay admiration, and while money is spent free-handedly out of the great abundance, and while all the squares and streets are brilliant with flowers and tapestries and illumination, and alive with carriages and pedestrians, then Israel sits in the gloom of its dark ghetto with no share in the merriment of the festival and in the sweat of his brow sews at the rags piled before his door.

But now come his own festivals, and the poor peddler lays his rubbish aside, puts on his best clothes, and raises his stooped form erect. It is precisely here, I believe, that the profoundest poetry of the festival and its highest meaning are to be found, because the celebrant raises himself from the slave fetters of his workaday toil and from his dusty wretchedness and is transformed into ideal humanity, which belongs not to his cramped chamber nor to his dismal breadwinning but to the universe. Then does this singular people assemble in festive array, and wherever they may reside, in whatever distant and hostile corner of the earth, they look upon one another as the ancient people of Israel, as the children of Abraham and Jacob and the flower of mankind which God's own hand has planted in the world. I attended the Passover festival in the ghetto. I came to know of the day by chance, for as I was walking through the ghetto I saw cauldrons scoured clean before every door and dishes being cleansed at every fountain. I was told that this was done for the Easter festival, which was to be celebrated in a few days. The Jewish Easter commemorates the exodus from Egypt. For this wondrous people it is the festival of an ideal liberation, and a solace and a prophecy, especially in the bondage of the ghetto.

After the great church solemnities of Carnival and Easter week at St. Peter's and the Sistine Chapel, which in the union of such grandiose achievements and magnificent forces mark the highest attainment of the Christian cult, it is fascinating to attend an Easter ceremony in the gloomy ghetto and to find the hoary and scarcely altered bases for the Catholic cult of Rome. They are the roots of that cult, and the more magnificent the development of the tree the deeper are its roots buried in the night.

The festival was celebrated in the synagogue. I have already said that the synagogue of the Jews of Rome is situated opposite the palace of the Cenci. It combines five schools (or congregations) in a single house, namely the Scuola del Tempio, Catalana, Castigliana, and the Scuola Nuova.* This indicates that the Roman ghetto is divided into five dioceses or parishes, of which each represents a separate character according to the prevailing nationality of the Jews, whose ancestors were either of ancient Roman origin or derived from Spain and Sicily. I was told that

* [Epigraphical evidence supplies the names of thirteen synagogues of the classical period. In 1520 we know there were eleven, some doubtless continuations, under different names, of the ancient congregations, some formed by exiles from France and Spain in the 14th and 15th centuries. By the end of the 16th century the number was reduced to the five which Gregorovius mentions; his enumeration omits the Sicilian congregation. The building which Gregorovius describes is that of the del Tempio synagogue, the largest of the five, as reconstructed after the fire of 1268.—*Tr.*]

the parish of Tempio more than any of the other Hebrews claimed descent from the Jews before Titus. Each synagogue has its school, in which children are taught the barest elements of reading, writing, and arithmetic; but no science is taught. Each also has its own sanctuary, in which the Pentateuch is kept. I saw these temple rooms at the Easter festival. The ghetto has wrung gold and silver from itself in order to fit out a Mosaic house. From the outside the synagogue reveals its character not only by inscriptions but by its peculiar architecture. In Rome, where temples and churches spread themselves abroad with conspicuous grandeur, the Jews have virtually built their house of God by stealth and decorated it surreptitiously. It appears that they have appropriated out of the abundance of Roman marbles fragments of a brace of pillars and capitals and a few pieces of marble in order to build them silently into their sanctuary. The small entablature at the middle of the synagogue building is decorated with Corinthian columns and shows that the Roman style has penetrated even into the ghetto. The stucco frieze boasts a likeness of the seven-branched candelabrum, the harp of David, and the zither of Miriam.

A scholar invited me to spend the evening in

the temple hall, where, as he said, vespers would be sung and I would be able to hear an excellently performed oratorio. In the evening all the Jewish people crowded at the entrance of the synagogue. There were also some Romans, even several priests, to be noticed in the throng. We were made to wait a half hour before the doors were opened; I was no little pleased to wait and see others waiting because it amused me to see this mark of sovereignty practiced for once by an oppressed and despised group. When the doors were opened we climbed a narrow stair into the hall. I have seen the stately synagogue of Livorno, perhaps the richest in the world; but it seemed far less remarkable to me than this room in the Roman ghetto. The building in Livorno is large, distinguished, and sober; the rooms in Rome are small, quite old, very colorful, bizarre, and foreign. Quite after the manner of the Catholic churches of Rome when festivals are being celebrated, the walls of the room were hung with tapestries embroidered in scarlet and gold, and the columns were covered with damask. Numerous quotations from the Old Testament were embroidered on the hangings. The ceiling was coffered after the fashion of the Roman basilicas, but decorated only with painted ornaments. The frieze which encircled the room bore a stucco relief which represented the Temple and all the vessels appropriate to the cult; it was interesting to see them here in Rome, where some of them are represented on the Arch of Titus. There was the Temple of Solomon, artistically represented, with all its gates, side halls, and altars, the brazen sea, the sacred Ark with the cherubim, and the priestly vestments and tiara, the original patterns of episcopal and papal costumes. There was every manner of Temple vessel, pots, bowls, and ladles, basins, spoons and pans, stools, and, finally, all the musical instruments: timbrels, tambourines, harps, zithers, flutes, jubilee trumpets, bagpipes, cymbals, and also the sistrum of the Egyptian Isis, which is so often to be seen on Isis monuments in the Vatican. It was with these reminiscences of the Temple in Jerusalem that the fantasy of the Jews had here surrounded themselves.

On the north wall there was a striking round window divided into twelve fields of various colors; this symbol represents the tribes of Israel, and is the likeness of the Urim and Tummim, the ornament fitted together of precious stones, which the High Priest used to wear upon his breast. To the west was a round choir, a wooden desk for cantor and singers, and upon it the silver temple candelabra and other remarkable vessels of silver which were fixed to the Pentateuch for ornament. Opposite, at the east wall, was the sanctuary, a small temple entablature with projecting rods (designed for carrying the Ark of the Covenant) resting upon Corinthian columns. The sanctuary was covered with a curtain, upon which was embroidered, in gold, inscriptions and various designs composed of roses and ornamental arabesques after the manner of the Temple of Solomon. The summit of the whole was crowned by a silver seven-armed candelabrum. In this sanctuary the Pentateuch is kept, a large parchment scroll. It is carried in procession through the hall and is displayed to the four points of the compass, whereupon the Jews raise their arms and utter a cry. This is so to speak the Monstrance and Host of the Jews. It is the mightiest God of the earth, who still holds the world fettered, the God who is not the Word but the Letter, a fearful, positive, and inexorable God of slavery. Judaism is the most positive of all religions, and therefore it endures to this day. Compared to the luxuriant forms and fanciful ceremonies of the Catholic Church, this stark, imageless, unfanciful and unfigured service of Jehovah seems admirable in its absolute simplicity and awe-inspiring sublimity, in the dispassionate despotism of the Law, which devours both the spirit of man and nature without pity.

Their heads covered with hat or cap, the Jews sit in the temple like peers before their God, or as if they were at the bourse. During the singing and praying there is little decorum; everyone sings when he chooses, or chats with his neighbor. The cantor, meanwhile, sits upon a raised choir. I was struck by the speed with which all these prayers were chanted or mumbled. The women sit in an upper gallery, behind a lattice as in a harem, and are not visible.

Vespers were sung in another hall. This too was decorated with finery and glittered with many lights. Its ceiling was not flat as in the first hall but was raised by stages into a bizarre kind of dome. In the choir the choristers sat behind the precentor. The latter wore a black gown and a tall black sacerdotal beret from which a white scarf fell on either side. The simplicity of this garb struck me as I thought of the old Jewish priestly vestments whose marvelous elegance is preserved in the papal garb. The High Priest in the Temple of Jerusalem must have surpassed even the pope in the magnificence of his attire. Whenever he entered the Holy of Holies he was swathed in a linen robe over which a fringed outer garment of hyacinth blue billowed. Golden bells alternating with pomegranates hung from the fringes. The outer garment was fastened by a sash of five girdles, of gold, purple, hyacinth, scarlet, and byssus. In addition he wore upon his shoulders a garment of the same colors but rich in gold and fastened by gold and sardonyx brooches in the form of a shield. Upon his breast were the Urim and Tummim with twelve precious stones. Upon his head he wore the tiara of byssus picked out with hyacinth, and around the tiara was a golden fillet inscribed "Jehovah." So Josephus describes the costume of the High Priest, and it is easy to see that his appearance must have been impressive enough.

The choristers sang the vespers quite well indeed, while the precentor prayed during the pauses, hiding his face in his scarf to express bitter weeping. The songs were harmonious, yet not in the ancient mode, but rather modern and in the style of the oratorio. There were beautiful boys' voices and magnificent bassos; even this ghetto vesper showed the influence of Rome and even the Jews could exhibit a *Miserere*. These people felt no little exultation and satisfaction in being able to produce an artistic work in their nook. Praise offered was accepted with visible joy. The visitor, near whom a Jewish lad had taken his position, was delighted to hear his heartily expressed praise being spread further. "What did he say?" "He said, 'Excellently done, *ben bene, eccellentissime;* you have a Sistine Chapel here.'"

But here we break off. It would be well if these pages might encourage some expert to undertake a thorough account of the history of the Jews of Rome. This section of Roman antiquity is better worth writing about than many a sterile research. Accompanying as it does the development of Roman Christianity from the earliest times, the history of the ghetto might well lend itself to making complete a section of the history of civilization in general.

The author was attracted to this subject not by the question of Jewish civil rights, but only by the glaring contrast between historical Judaism and historical Christianity here in Rome. The character of this city of cities as it presents itself to the modern observer bears the imprint of three great periods in the culture of the human race: Judaism, classical antiquity, and Christianity. They can hardly be distinguished from one another, so intricately have they grown together, so much that is Jewish and classical has the Christian cult incorporated in itself. If one wanders through Rome and its splendors and leaves aside the sights of antiquity, everywhere the spirit and form of Hebraism strike the eye, even in the pinnacles of Christian art. In sculpture we have Michelangelo's *Moses* on the tomb of Pope Julius II, the noblest production in marble of the Christian genius. In painting Raphael's *Stanze* and loggias, the Sistine Chapel, and countless other examples are filled with representations from the Bible of the Jews. In music the noblest and profoundest chants of Holy Week, the *Lamentations* and the *Miserere,* are the Lamentations of Jeremiah and the Psalms of the Jews. And of this people, to which fate has entrusted the charters of mankind and which Christianity has so to speak displaced from its heritage, there dwell here in the ghetto one of the oldest and historically most remarkable remnants, upon which history has enacted its great and tragic irony. But this despised people has enacted its own irony on the political world, for to the other symbols of its religion it has added an additional symbol, powerful in political history; and that is the Golden Calf, about which the world eager to borrow dances, as is presaged, inscribed, and described in the books of Moses the Prophet.

Translator's Postscript

FERDINAND GREGOROVIUS, historian of the medieval periods of the two great cities of antiquity, Rome and Athens, was born in 1821 in Eastern Prussia. He was educated for the ministry but soon turned to the study of history and philosophy. Stirred by the ideas of 1848, he was especially interested in the national independence of oppressed peoples. Among his earliest works are an essay, "The Idea of Polish Nationality," and two series of "Polish and Magyar Songs." Similarly, his interest in post-classical Italian and Greek history was first stimulated by the movement for Italian and Greek independence which was active in his time.

In 1852 Gregorovius went to Italy where he resided continuously until 1874. It was there that he composed his eight-volume history, *Rome in the Middle Ages,* and it is of this long sojourn that his *Wanderjahre in Italien* give a beautiful account. The essay on the Roman ghetto, here translated, has been taken from the *Wanderjahre.*

The Ghetto and the Jews of Rome was written in 1853 in the second year of his long Roman residence. How the thirty-two-year-old author came to be attracted to this theme so soon after he first confronted the Eternal City, he has himself indicated in the moving stanzas of his poem and in several passages of his essay. The proximity of the ghetto to the Arch of Titus and to so many other sites recalling the tragedy of the Jewish people, appeared to him as a symbolic representation of an enigma of history, the mystery of how the Jews had been able to survive when the glorious civilization of their conquerors had faded and died. Gregorovius, of course, had the advantage of writing at a time when the centuries-old ghetto was still to be seen. A few decades later the Roman Jews were emancipated (1870), and in 1885 the old ghetto disappeared.

Gregorovius wandered through the Roman ghetto as if he were browsing in a great hall of antiquity. Jewish spiritual life was alien to him and he did not trouble to find out what in its inner life had been able to motivate and sustain the unchanging existence of the community. He was moved by the spectacle more than by the desires and convictions, the hopes and strivings, the living faith which had been able to surmount all external disasters. This static approach may account for certain curious errors of fact. Thus, for example, Gregorovius derives the word "ghetto" from the talmudic *get*, which he takes to mean "separation." The talmudic word originally meant "document" and was applied to a bill of divorce. Moreover, he also declared in his essay that the Ark of the Covenant was displayed in Titus' triumphal procession through Rome. Actually it had been destroyed together with the First Temple. There are other such lapses of accuracy, and although they seem trivial, it is surprising to find them in a scholar of such stature.

Gregorovius' suggestion (in the penultimate paragraph of the present essay) that fuller attention be given to the study of the Jews of Rome has been followed. Aside from numerous special studies and the accounts in general histories, a number of books have dealt specifically with the history of the Jews of Rome. For the English reader the most convenient is Hermann Vogelstein's *Rome* (Philadelphia 1940). In German there are two substantive works, both somewhat antiquated: A. Berliner, *Geschichte der Juden in Rom von den aeltesten Zeiten bis zur Gegenwart* (Frankfort on the Main 1893), and H. Vogelstein and P. Rieger, *Geschichte der Juden in Rom* (Berlin 1895-1896). Progress has been made in understanding the social and economic life of the ghetto, and the organization and character of the Jewish community in antiquity. For the first, the papers of A. Milano in *Rassegna Mensile di Israel* 6-9 (1930-1934) are illuminating. For the second, special mention might be made of Jean Juster, *Les Juifs dans l'Empire Romain* (Paris 1914); George La Piana, "Foreign Groups in Rome during the First Centuries of the Empire," reprinted from the *Harvard Theological Review* 20 (1927); and H. J. Leon's studies on the Jewish catacombs in *Transactions and Proceedings of the American Philological Association* 58 and 59 (1927-1928). A conspectus of all monuments and antiquities of Rome which relate to Jews and Judaism is to be found in Ermanno Loevinson, *Roma Israelitica: Wanderungen eines Juden durch die Kunststaetten Roms* (Frankfort on the Main 1927). A scholarly history of the Jews of Italy (in which the Jews of Rome are of course treated) is Cecil Roth, *The History of the Jews of Italy* (Philadelphia 1946).

Chronology

The Jews in Rome

B.C.E.

- 161 Visit of envoys of Judah the Maccabee to Rome
- 139 Expulsion of Jews from Rome and Italy by Praetor Hispalus (first indication of the presence of Jews in Rome)
- 63 Capture of Jerusalem by Pompey; large contingents of Jewish prisoners of war brought to Rome
- 37 Visit of Herod to Rome and his designation as King of Judea by the Consuls and Senate
- 3 Jewish embassy visits Rome, seeking removal of Herodian dynasty; escorted to Imperial Palace by 8,000 Roman Jews

C.E.

- 19 Sejanus' banishment of the Jews from Italy
- 40 Philo's mission to Caligula
- 49–51 Claudius' banishment of the Jews from Rome
- 61 Apostle Paul in Rome
- 66–70 [Jewish War in Palestine]
- 70 [Fall of Jerusalem]
  Introduction of the *Fiscus Judaicus*, special tax levied on Jews
- 93 Publication of Josephus' *Jewish Antiquities*
- 132–35 [Bar Kokhba revolt]
  Hadrian prohibits practice of Judaism as subversive to the state; regulations not enforced in Rome
- *after* 135 Palestinian talmudic master Mattia ben Heresh establishes House of Study in Rome
- 204 Emperor Septimius Severus forbids conversion to Christianity or Judaism
- 212 Edict of Emperor Caracalla, extending Roman citizenship to all free inhabitants of the Empire
- 270–75 Rome fortified by Emperor Aurelian, drawing the Trastevere within the walls

313 Constantine the Great, converted to Christianity, issues Edict of Milan, proclaiming equal rights for all religions

330 [Byzantium, rebuilt and renamed Constantinople, made capital of the Empire]

362 Emperor Julian checks Christian persecution of heretics and expresses intention to rebuild Temple at Jerusalem

410 Rome sacked by Alaric and the Visigoths

435 Roman law codified by Theodosius II Systematization of all anti-Jewish legislation enacted since Constantine

455 Rome sacked by the Vandals

476 Deposition of Emperor Romulus Augustulus by the German Odoacer—end of Roman Empire

500 Theodoric the Great, King of the Goths, confirms Jews in their privileges

509–604 Initiation of a papal Jewish policy by Gregory the Great

756 Donation of Pepin, King of the Franks, establishes Papal States (*Patrimonium Petri*)

1073–85 Pope Gregory VII (Hildebrand); forbids Jews to hold positions of authority over Christians

1101 Completion of *Arukh,* great lexicographical work by Nathan ben Yehiel of Rome

1120 Pope Calixtus II issues bull for protection of the Jews

1130–37 Anacletus II (Cardinal Pierleone, son of a converted Jew), the "Jewish Pope"

1140 Abraham ibn Ezra of Spain in Rome

1166 Benjamin of Tudela of Spain visits Rome

1179 Third Lateran Council renews anti-Jewish legislation

1215 Fourth Lateran Council decrees anti-Jewish

	legislation; Jews required to wear identifying badges
1239	Pope Gregory IX orders confiscation of Talmud
1247	Pope Innocent IV issues bull against ritual-murder charge
1257	Pope Alexander IV renews ordinance requiring wearing of Jews' badge in Papal States
1267	Pope Ciement IV issues bull requiring Inquisition to proceed with severity against Jews attempting to influence converts
1270	Birth of Immanuel ben Solomon ha-Romi; physician, Bible exegete, poet, member of circle around Dante; author of Dantean poem, *Hell and Paradise*
1277–80	Pope Nicolas III institutes conversionist sermons
1305–78	Avignon period of the papacy
1310	Republican government of Rome (Cola di Rienzo) extends protective privileges to the Jews
1322	Burning of Talmud by papal order
1402	Pope Boniface IX's bull of protection renews and extends privileges granted Jews by Roman Republic
1417–31	Pope Martin V (Otto Colonna); issues bull of protection and, later, bull subsuming Jews under law of citizens
1442	Papal bull of persecution, depriving Jews of virtually all rights
1466	Pope Paul II introduces Roman Carnival; beginning of Jewish footraces
before 1480	Printing of important Hebrew incunabula (*e.g.*, Rashi's Commentary on the Pentateuch, *Arukh* by Nathan ben Yehiel, Nahmanides' Commentary on the Pentateuch, *Mishneh Torah* by Maimonides), supposedly in Rome
1524	Reorganization of Jewish community by Daniel ben Isaac da Pisa; approved by papal brief

David Reubeni, the false Messiah, received by Pope

1527 Sack of Rome by Charles V; destruction of Jewish community

1533-43 Widmanstad studies Kabbalah in Rome under Jewish teachers; acquires important Kabbalist manuscripts

1539 Establishment of a *Mons Pietatis* in Rome by ecclesiastical authorities to combat Jewish moneylending

1543 House of Catechumens established for Jewish initiates to Christianity; later supported by special tax levied on Jewish community

1553 Burning of Hebrew books on the Campo dei Fiori

1555 Cardinal Caraffa mounts the papal throne as Paul IV; proclamation of the papal bull *Cum nimis absurdum*, confining Jews to a walled ghetto, restricting Jewish communities to one synagogue in each city, forbidding Jews to own land, and requiring Jewish badge to be worn

1557 Confiscation and burning of Jewish books

1564 Permission granted to print Talmud

1569 Pius V's bull *Hebraeorum gens*, expelling Jews from all Papal States except Rome and Ancona

1577 Institution of conversionist sermons by Pope Gregory XIII

1585 Pope Sixtus V permits return of Jews expelled from Papal States

1593 Clement VIII again expels Jews from all Papal States except Rome and Ancona

1601 Pope Clement VIII orders confiscation and burning of Talmud

1611 Pope Paul V deprives Jews of civil jurisdiction

1661 Adoption of sumptuary legislation, the *Pragmatica*, by the Jewish congregation

1668   Pope Clement IX abolishes Carnival footraces, replacing them by humiliating ceremony of homage before Conservatori of city

1733   New anti-Jewish code drawn up under Pope Clement XII

1758   Cardinal Lorenzo Ganganelli, the future Clement XIV, draws up memorandum against ritual-murder accusation

1775   Pius VI mounts papal throne; issues *Editto sopra gli ebrei,* summarization of all persecutory measures of his predecessors

1793   Attack on ghetto by Roman mob after assassination of representative of French Republic

1798   General Berthier enters Rome; abolishes all special legislation
Jews declared citizens with equal rights
Roman Republic proclaimed
Rome recaptured by Neapolitans

1800   Modified papal regime reinstated

1808   French dissolve papal rule

1814   Downfall of Napoleon followed by reconstitution of Papal States

1815   Return of Pope Pius VII from exile
Ghetto re-established

1823–29   Pope Leo XII revives edict of 1775; conversionist sermons reintroduced

1831–46   Pope Gregory XVI revives Carnival impost on Jews

1848   Walls and gates of ghetto razed on order of Pope Pius IX; abolition of conversionist sermons

1849   Proclamation of Roman Republic by National Assembly
Restoration of papal rule by European powers
Return of Pius IX; ghetto re-established

1858 Mortara case (abduction and forced conversion of a Jewish boy)
1861 Kingdom of Italy proclaimed by first Italian parliament
1870 Troops of Kingdom of Italy take Rome, completing unification of Italy
Abolition of ghetto